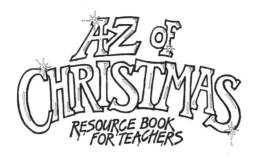

A-Z of CHRISTMAS

RESOURCE BOOK FOR TEACHERS

D1299657

A-Z of CHRISTMAS

RESOURCE BOOK FOR TEACHERS

VIRGINIA FERGUSON   PETER DURKIN

M

Copyright © Virginia Ferguson and Peter Durkin 1991

Project commissioned and managed by
Lorraine Bambrough-Kelly, The Writer's Style

Cover design and illustration by Ian Forss
Designed by Jennifer Peta Richardson
Illustrations by Jennifer Peta Richardson

All rights reserved
No part of this publication may be reproduced or transmitted
in any form or by any means without permission

First published 1991 by
THE MACMILLAN COMPANY OF AUSTRALIA PTY LTD
107 Moray Street, South Melbourne 3205
6 Clarke Street, Crows Nest 2065

Associated companies
and representatives throughout the world

National Library of Australia
cataloguing in publication data

Ferguson, Virginia
    A-Z of Christmas : a resource book for teachers

    ISBN 0 7329 1265 2

1. Christmas — Study and teaching (Primary)
I. Durkin, Peter   II. Title

372.8

Set in Universe by Cherry Graphics

Printed in Hong Kong

Acknowledgements
The publisher wishes to thank the following for permission to
reproduce the copyright material:
Penguin Books Ltd for *Holidays* from *Songs for my dog and other people* by Max Fatchen
(Kestrel Books, 1980) copyright © Max Fatchen, 1980 and *The Rabbit's Christmas Carol* from
Hot Dog and Other Poems by Kit Wright (Kestrel Books, 1981) copyright © Kit Wright, 1981;
Miss D.E. Collins (represented by A.P. Watt and Son) for *How far is it to Bethlehem?* by Frances
Chesterton; Wes Magee for *Questions on Christmas Eve* by Wes Magee from *A Third Poetry
Book* Oxford, 1982; Faber & Faber for *Kings Came Riding* by Charles Williams from *The Faber
Book of Nursery Verse*; the poet and the publisher (represented by David Higham Associates for
High in the Heaven (Charles Causley); the Trustees for the Copyrights of the late Dylan Thomas
and J.M. Dent & Sons, for the extract from *Quite Early One Morning* by Dylan Thomas.

Introduction

A-Z of Christmas provides you with a wide variety of things to make and do with your class in the weeks leading up to Christmas. Be prepared for your Christmas celebrations by choosing from these simple activities. All are presented with clear diagrams and step-by-step instructions.

There are ideas for:

- Tree decorations
- Entertaining visitors
- Food
- Table presentation
- Decorations
- Christmas cards
- Presents
- Wrapping paper
- Games

Merry Christmas!

Virginia and Peter

Contents

Alphabets for Christmas

Design your own Christmas alphabet.

1 Draw 26 squares (about 2.5 x 2.5cm each) of equal size onto heavy card.

2 Design each letter around a Christmas symbol. They might look like this.

3 Fill in with bright, strong colours and decorate with glitter.

4 Cut out each square, then string the letters together to make a large and colourful happy Christmas sign. You might need to make more than just one of some letters.

Advent Calendar

1 Photocopy the calendar and give one to each child. The larger the calendar the better, so use the enlarger on the photocopier.

2 Draw a Christmas scene in each square.

3 Cut out 25 windows, each to fit a picture square.

4 Stick each window onto the side of a picture square like this

5 Number the windows 1-25.

6 As each day passes fold a window back to show a picture.

Note: To look really effective mount each calendar on card or a colourful piece of cover paper.

glue here
fold

Bells, Balls, Beads and Baubles

Folded bells

1 Fold a square of paper or thin card in half.

2 Draw half a bell design, like this.

3 Cut out around bell.

4 Hang or pin up.

A line of bells

1 Fold a longer, thinner piece of paper into a fan shape.

2 Draw half a bell shape, as shown.

3 Cut out BUT be careful — DO NOT CUT the right-hand edge.

4 Open out. Paint or decorate.

5 Hang or pin up.

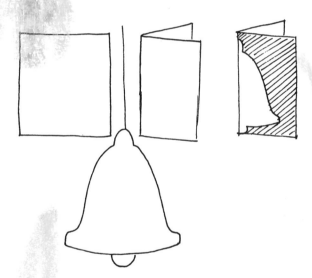

Paper strip balls

1 Cut four strips of coloured paper (or foil) 20cm long and 1cm wide. (Or you can use your own sized strips.)

2 Lay the four strips across each other and staple through the centre, like this.

3 Take each end and bring up to the top. Overlap. Staple or glue all strips.

4 Hang ball by a thread.

Balloon balls

1 Blow up a balloon and tie or knot tightly.

2 Cover the surface with PVA glue.

3 Gently wrap string or bright wool round and round the balloon. Make an interesting criss-crossy pattern.

4 Let the glue dry.

5 Pop the balloon and hang up your new decoration. Make a few more.

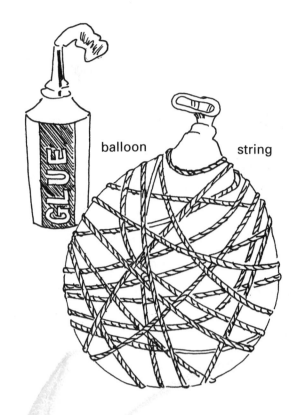

balloon   string

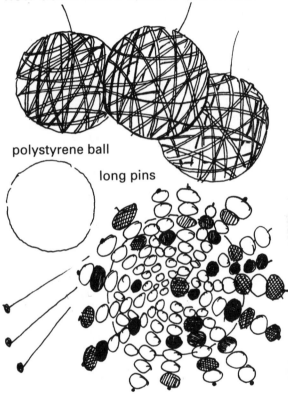

polystyrene ball

long pins

Beaded baubles

1 You will need polystyrene balls, long pins and tiny beads.

2 Thread beads on long pins.

3 Poke pins into polystyrene balls.

4 Keep adding pins and beads until the ball is covered.

5 Hang on tree.

Pipe cleaner baubles

1 Twist coloured pipe cleaners into Christmas shapes.

* Make a star shape and hang a small lolly inside. Make a bell shape, and do the same.

* Make any other shapes you can think of — musical instruments, trees, parcels, reindeer, angels . . .

2 Attach string or cotton and hang on tree.

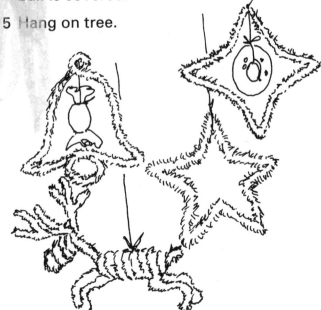

Egg carton baubles

1 Cut two sections from an egg carton.

2 Make a hole through the bottom of each section and pull a thread with a knot in the end through both (so you can hang the bauble up). You could use a bead instead of a knot.

3 Glue the two parts together.

4 Paint with poster paint and decorate with glitter, beads or sequins.

5 Hang up singly or link several.

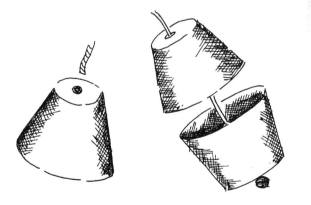

Matchbox baubles

1 Place a small present in the tray of a matchbox, e.g. a few small coins (a cent, if you're poor; $2, if you're rich!), some lollies, a tiny toy or model, a trinket or two.

2 Cover the matchbox with pretty wrapping paper (or use coloured paper decorated with glitter).

3 Tie to the tree.

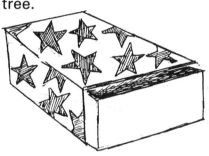

Biscuits and Shortbread

Iced biscuits

You will need:

250g plain flour
125g butter
125g brown sugar
1 egg, beaten
pinch of salt

1 Beat butter and sugar together until fluffy.

2 Mix in the egg a little at a time.

3 Sift in flour and salt. Mix well.

4 Roll out dough on floured board to 1/2cm thickness.

5 Cut into Christmas shapes with cutters.

6 Cook biscuits on greased trays in oven at 190°C, for about 15 minutes.

7 Ice and decorate. You can make icing by mixing icing sugar and hot water together until smooth, then adding drops of food colouring.

Christmas shortbread

You will need:

150g plain flour
100g butter
 50g sugar

1 Sift sugar and flour into a mixing bowl.

2 Rub butter into flour and sugar until it looks something like breadcrumbs.

3 Roll the dough into a ball.

4 Take a piece of the dough and roll it into a squared finger shape. Flatten it gently with a fork. (Make it about 1cm thick.)

5 Place finished shortbread fingers on a greased baking tray and cook in the oven at 170°C for 20 minutes.

6 Turn the oven down to 150°C and continue cooking for another 20-25 minutes, until golden brown.

7 Cool.

Bon-Bons

These cost the earth in the shops and we always find them very disappointing!
Try making some better ones of your own.

1 Make a paper tube.

2 Cut through nearly all of the middle of the tube (to make it easier to pull apart). Leave about 15mm uncut.

3 Write some jokes or riddles on a piece of paper. Include one in each bon-bon. Place a lolly or two and a trinket inside the tube. (Make sure these goodies don't fall in the middle slit.)

4 Cover tube with bright crepe paper. Leave 6-8cm hanging over each end, to be bunched up.

5 Decorate with stars, shapes, tinsel or Christmas stickers.

6 Tie the ends up tightly (as shown).

7 Test one with a friend.

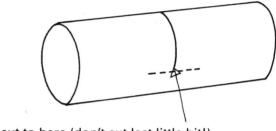

cut to here (don't cut last little bit!)

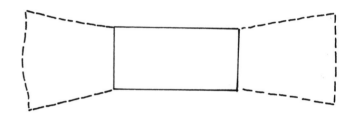

Cards from Oil-pastel Rubbings

Leaf rubbings

1 Place a leaf with the veins facing up underneath a sheet of paper.

2 Rub the side of an oil pastel or wax crayon over the paper (move it from side to side) until the design shows through.

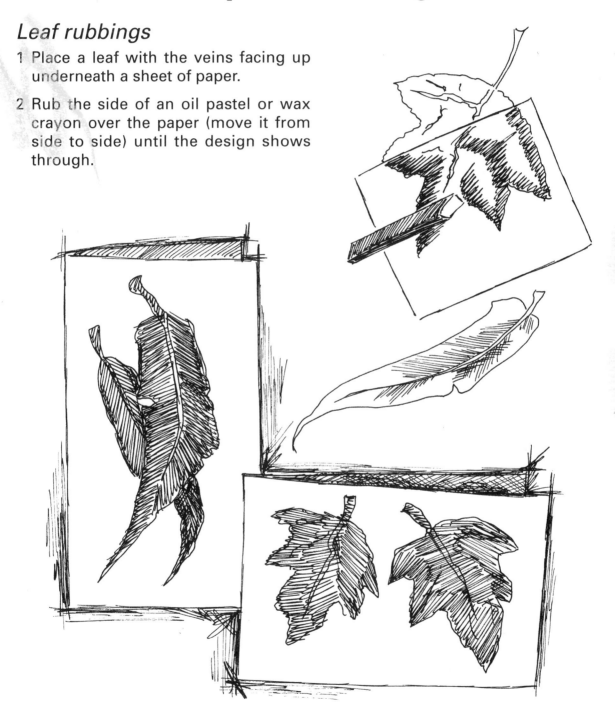

Christmas shape rubbings

1 Cut a Christmas shape from card.

2 Use the shape as a template to cut another the same size.

3 Stick them together. (This gives a higher raised surface and makes the rubbing more effective.)

4 Place this shape under a sheet of plain paper and rub the side of an oil pastel across the shape until it shows through.

5 Cut out your rubbings and stick them to card.

OR

1 Make a more interesting picture by sticking card shapes on to a firmer backing card.

2 Place the front of a blank folded card on top of the design (or to the backing sheet with the shapes). Use masking tape to keep steady.

3 Gently rub the surface with the sides of oil pastels. Try different colours and designs.

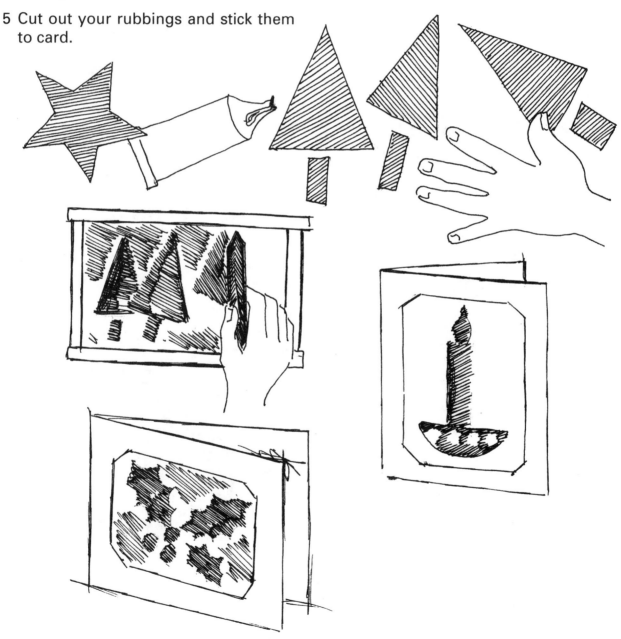

Chains

The simplest chain of all

1 Cut some strips of coloured paper.

2 Make one strip into a circle using staples or glue.

3 Thread each strip through another, making a chain as shown. Staple or glue as you go.

4 Keep on going until your chain is long enough.

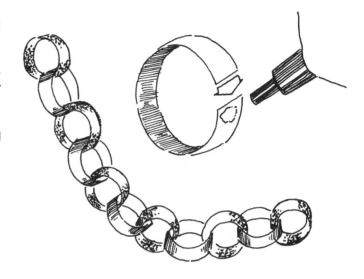

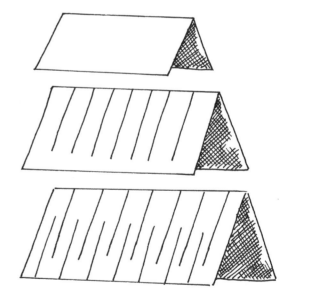

Cut and pull-out folded chain

1 Fold a piece of coloured paper like this.

2 Cut from the fold to about 15mm from the edge.

3 Keep paper folded.
Now cut from the edge up to the fold.
DO NOT CUT THE FOLD.
Stop cutting 15mm from the fold.

4 Open the paper out flat. Carefully pull the ends apart.

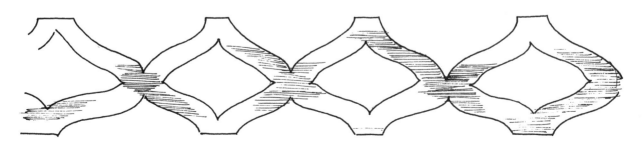

The sticking circles chain

1 Enlarge this circle on the photocopier, then photocopy it or trace it 30 or 40 times.

2 Cut out the centre part.

3 Staple each side of a circle to the next one.

4 Then staple in the opposite direction — on top of this circle and stick the next one to it.

5 Keep on going until your chain is long enough.

Note: You could try using glue instead of staples but we found it didn't work very well.

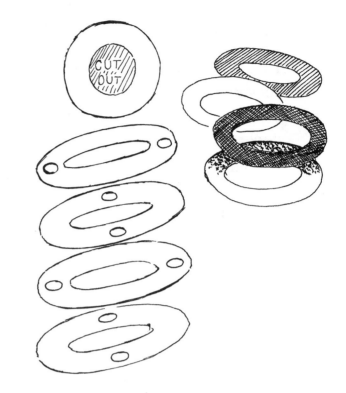

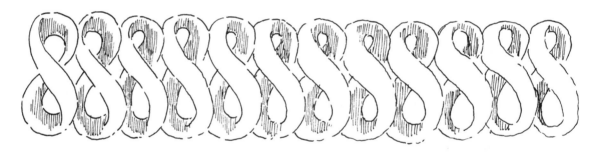

A fan-shape chain

1 Fold a l-o-n-g strip of coloured paper into a fan shape.

2 Trace or draw a pattern, for example a tree, bell or angel, on the top piece of paper.

3 Cut away the excess part.

4 Cut through EVERY piece of paper and be careful not to cut the sides.

5 Unfold the paper.

6 If you want an even longer chain, join five or six lots together.

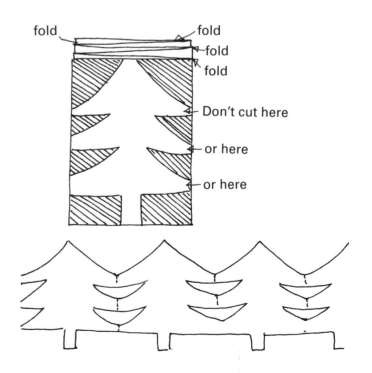

A pleated chain

1 You will need two long strips of different coloured paper, say a white and a red.

2 Take the red strip and place it across the white one like this.

3 Fold the white strip up.

4 Fold the red strip across to the right.

5 Fold the white one down.

6 Fold the red one across to the left.

7 After this, just repeat the pattern.

   white up, red right
   white down, red left
   white up, red right
   white down, red left
   and so on.

8 You will finish with a chain like this.

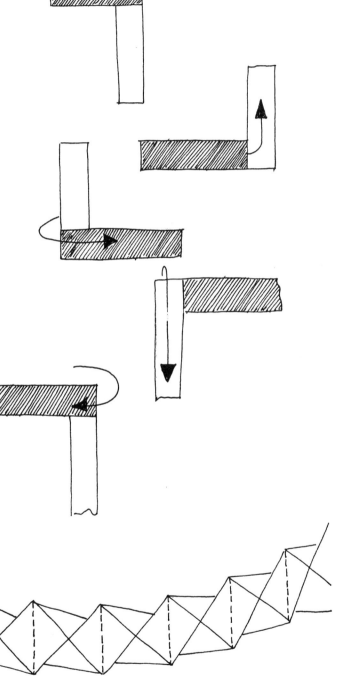

Christmas Calligraphy Patterns, Pictures and Borders

Use these to create your own Christmas posters, cards, letters and artwork.

'TIS THE SEASON

Merry Christmas

NOEL

Greetings

Christmas cheer

NOEL

BUON NATALE

Joy to the world

Christmas Carol Collection

As a special treat organise a class Carols by Candlelight-type concert and booklet. Invite along other classes and parents and friends, too.

O little Town of Bethlehem

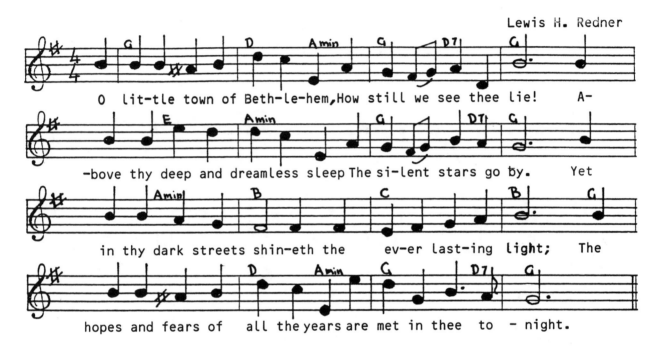

Lewis H. Redner

O lit-tle town of Beth-le-hem, How still we see thee lie! A-
-bove thy deep and dreamless sleep The si-lent stars go by. Yet
in thy dark streets shin-eth the ev-er last-ing light; The
hopes and fears of all the years are met in thee to-night.

2 For Christ is born of Mary
  And gathered all above,
  While mortals sleep, the angels keep
  Their watch of wond'ring love.
  O morning stars, together,
  Proclaim the holy Birth,
  And praises sing to God our King,
  And peace to men on earth.

Away in a Manger

Martin Luther

A - way in a man-ger, no crib for a bed, the
Lit-tle Lord Jes - us lay down His sweet head. The
stars in the bright sky look'd down where He lay, The
lit-tle Lord Jes - us, a - sleep in the hay.

2 The cattle are lowing, the Baby awakes;
The little Lord Jesus, no crying He makes
I love Thee, Lord Jesus, look down from the sky,
And stay by my cradle till morning is nigh.

The First Noel

Traditional English

The first No-el the an-gel did say Was to
cer-tain poor shep-herds in fields as they lay, In
fields where they lay keep-ing their sheep On a
cold win-ter's night that was so deep No-
-el, No-el, No-el, No-el,
Born is the King of Is-ra-el.

2 They looked up and saw a star
Shining in the East beyond them far,
And to the earth it gave forth great light,
And so it continued both day and night.
Noel, Noel, Noel, Noel,
Born is the King of Israel.

3 Then let us all with one accord
   Sing praises to our Heavenly Lord,
   Who hath made heaven and earth of naught,
   And with His blood, mankind hath bought.
   Noel, Noel, Noel. Noel,
   Born is the King of Israel.

Hark! the Herald Angels Sing

Felix Mendelssohn

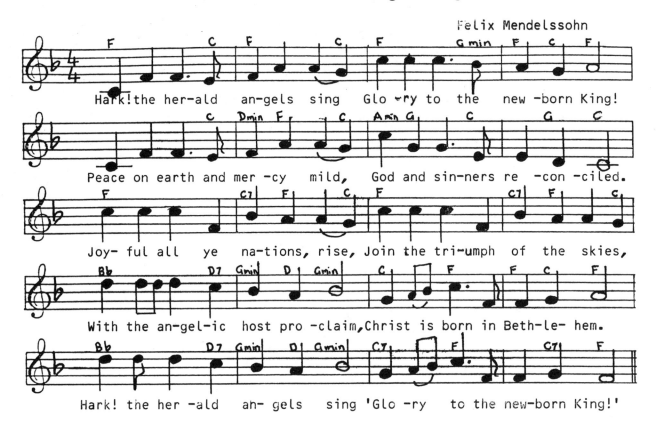

Hark! the her-ald an-gels sing Glo-ry to the new-born King!

Peace on earth and mer-cy mild, God and sin-ners re-con-ciled.

Joy-ful all ye na-tions, rise, Join the tri-umph of the skies,

With the an-gel-ic host pro-claim, Christ is born in Beth-le-hem.

Hark! the her-ald an-gels sing 'Glo-ry to the new-born King!!'

2 Hail, the heav'n-born Prince of Peace,
Hail, the Son of Righteousness;
Light and life to all He brings,
Ris'n with healing in His wings.
Mild, He lays His glory by,
Born that man no more may die;
Born to raise the sons of earth,
Born to give them second birth.
Hark! the herald angels sing,
Glory to the new-born King!

Now Sing We All Merrily

Old Welsh

Now sing we all mer -ri – ly, Christmas is here.

Day we love best of all days of the year.

We Three Kings

John H. Hopkins

We three kings of O - ri -ent are;

Bear - ing gifts we tra - verse a - far

Field and foun - tain, moor and moun - tain,

Fol- low-ing yon - der star: O_____

star of won - der, star of night,

Star with roy - al beau - ty bright,

West - ward lead - ing, Still pro - ceed - ing,

Guide us to thy per - fect light.

Melchior:

2 Born a King on Bethlehem's plain,
  Gold I bring to crown Him again,
  King forever, ceasing never,
  Over all to reign.

Refrain

Caspar:

3 Frankincense to offer have I,
  Incense owns a Deity nigh,
  Pray'r and praising, all men raising,
  Worship Him, God most high.

Refrain

Balthazar:

4 Myrrh is mine, its bitter perfume,
  Breathes a life of gathering gloom;
  Sorrowing, sighing, bleeding, dying,
  Seal'd in the stone-cold tomb.

Refrain

All

5 Glorious now behold Him arise,
  King and God and Sacrifice,
  Alleluia, Alleluia,
  Earth to the heav'ns replies.

Refrain.

Silent Night

Franz Gruber

Si - lent night, ho - ly night, All is calm, all is bright

Round yon Vir-gin mo-ther and child, Ho-ly in-fant so ten-der and mild

Sleep in heav-en-ly peace, _____ Sleep in heavenly peace. _____

2 Silent night, holy night,
Shepherds quake, at the sight;
Glories stream from heaven afar,
Heav'nly hosts sing Alleluia;
Christ, the Saviour, is born,
Christ, the Saviour, is born.

3 Silent night, holy night,
Son of God, love's pure light
Radiant beams from thy holy face,
With the dawn of redeeming grace,
Jesus, Lord, at thy birth,
Jesus, Lord, at thy birth.

Good King Wenceslas

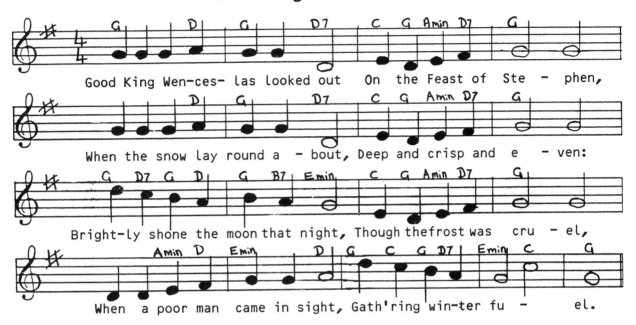

Good King Wen-ces- las looked out On the Feast of Ste - phen,
When the snow lay round a - bout, Deep and crisp and e - ven:
Bright-ly shone the moon that night, Though the frost was cru - el,
When a poor man came in sight, Gath'ring win-ter fu - el.

2 `Hither, page, and stand by me;
If thou know'st it, telling,
Yonder peasant, who is he,
Where and what his dwelling?'
`Sire, he lives a good league hence,
Underneath the mountain,
Right against the forest fence,
By Saint Agnes' fountain.'

3 `Bring me flesh, and bring me wine,
Bring me pine logs hither.
Thou and I shall see him dine,
When we bear them thither.'
Page and monarch forth they went,
Forth they went together;
Through the rude wind's wild lament,
And the bitter weather.

4 "Sire, the night is darker now
And the wind blows stronger.
Fails my heart, I know not how,
I can go no longer."
"Mark my footsteps my good page
Tread thou in them boldly,
Thou shalt find the bitter wind
Freeze thy blood less coldly.

5 In his master's steps he trod
Where the snow lay dinted
Heat was in the very sod
Which the saint had printed.
Therefore Christian men by sure
Wealth of rank possessing;
Yes who now will bless the poor
Shall yourself find blessing.

While shepherds watched

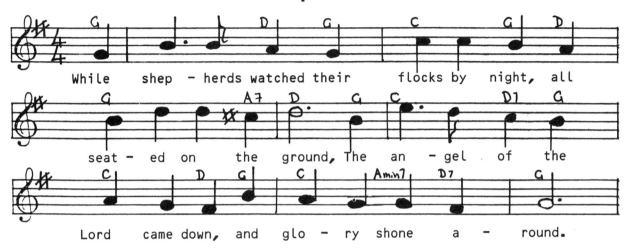

While shep - herds watched their flocks by night, all
seat - ed on the ground, The an - gel of the
Lord came down, and glo - ry shone a - round.

2 `Fear not', said he; for mighty dread
Had seized their troubled mind;
`Glad tidings of great joy I bring
To you and all mankind'.

3 `To you in David's town this day
Is born of David's line
A Saviour, who is Christ the Lord;
And this shall be the sign':

4 `The heavenly Babe you there shall find
   To human view displayed
   All meanly wrapped in swathing bands,
   And in a manger laid'.

5 Thus spake the Seraph, and forthwith
   Appeared a shining throng
   Of Angels praising God, who thus
   Addressed their joyful song:

6 `All glory be to God on high,
   And on the earth be peace;
   Good-will henceforth from heav'n to men
   Begin and never cease'.

The Twelve Days of Christmas

29

1 On the first day of Christmas
  my true love sent to me,
  a partridge in a pear tree.

2 On the second day of Christmas
  my true love sent to me,
  Two turtle doves,
  and a partridge in a pear tree.

3 On the third day of Christmas
my true love sent to me;
three French hens, two turtle doves,
and a partridge in a pear tree.

4 On the fourth day of Christmas
my true love sent to me,
four calling birds, three French hens,
two turtle doves and a partridge in a pear tree.

5 On the fifth day of Christmas
my true love sent to me,
five gold rings, four calling birds,
three French hens, two turtle doves,
and a partridge in a pear tree.

6 On the sixth day of Christmas
my true love sent to me,
six geese a-laying, five gold rings,
four calling birds, three French hens,
two turtle-doves, and a partridge in a pear tree.

7 On the seventh day of Christmas
my true love sent to me,
sev'n swans a-swimming, six geese a-laying,
five gold rings, four calling birds,
three French hens, two turtle doves,
and a partridge in a pear tree.

8 On the eighth day of Christmas
my true love sent to me,
eight maids a-milking, sev'n swans a-swimming,
six geese a-laying, five gold rings,
four calling birds, three French hens,
two turtle doves, and a partridge in a pear tree.

9 On the ninth day of Christmas
   my true love sent to me,
   nine ladies dancing, eight maids a-milking,
   sev'n swans a-swimming, six geese a-laying,
   five gold rings, four calling birds,
   three French hens,
   two turtle doves,
   and a partridge in a pear tree.

10 On the tenth day of Christmas,
   my true love sent to me,
   ten lords a-leaping, nine ladies dancing,
   eight maids a-milking, sev'n swans a-swimming,
   six geese a-laying, five gold rings,
   four calling birds, three French hens,
   two turtle doves, and a partridge in a pear tree.

11 On the eleventh day of Christmas
   my true love sent to me,
   elev'n pipers piping, ten lords a-leaping,
   nine ladies dancing, eight maids a-milking,
   sev'n swans a-swimming, six geese a-laying,
   five gold rings, four calling birds,
   three French hens, two turtle doves,
   and a partridge in a pear tree.

12 On the twelfth day of Christmas,
   my true love sent to me,
   twelve drummers drumming,
   elev'n pipers piping, ten lords a-leaping,
   nine ladies dancing, eight maids a-milking,
   sev'n swans a-swimming, six geese a-laying,
   five gold rings, four calling birds,
   three French hens, two turtle doves,
   and a partridge in a pear tree.

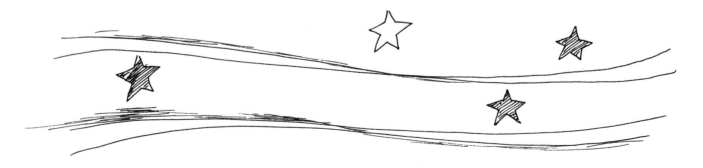

We Wish You a Merry Christmas

Refrain

Good tidings we bring to you and your kin;
We wish you a merry Christmas
And a happy New Year.

2 Now bring us some figgy pudding,
Now bring us some figgy pudding
Now bring us some figgy pudding,
And bring some out here.

Refrain

3 For we all like figgy pudding,
We all like figgy pudding,
We all like figgy pudding,
So bring some out here.

Refrain

Christmas Poems

Select some of these to be read or acted.

This is a poem as well as a carol.

One person reads the words clearly while the others hum the melody very quietly.

If the tune is not known, `Away in a Manger' fits in quite well.

Long, Long Ago

Winds through the olive trees,
Softly did blow,
Round little Bethlehem
Long, long ago.

Sheep on the hillside lay
Whiter than snow,
Shepherds were watching them,
Long, long ago.

Then from the happy sky,
Angels bent low,
Singing their songs of joy,
Long, long ago.

Then in a manger bed,
Cradled, we know,
Christ came to Bethlehem,
Long, long ago.

Traditional

Questions on Christmas Eve

But *how* can his reindeer fly without wings?
Jets on their hooves? That's plain cheating!
And *how* can he climb down the chimney pot
　When we've got central heating?

You say it's all magic and I shouldn't ask
About Santa on Christmas Eve.
But I'm confused by the stories I've heard;
　I don't know what to believe.

I said that I'd sit up in bed all night long
To see if he really would call.
But I fell fast asleep, woke up after dawn
　As something banged in the hall.

I saw my sock crammed with apples and sweets;
There were parcels piled high near the door.
Jingle bells tinkled far off in the dark;
　One snowflake shone on the floor.

Wes Magee

34

High in the Heaven

High in the Heaven
A gold star burns
Lighting our way
As the great world turns.

Silver the frost
It shines on the stem
As we now journey
To Bethlehem.

White is the ice
At our feet as we tread,
Pointing a path
To the manger-bed.

Charles Causley

Kings Came Riding

Kings came riding
  One, two and three,
Over the desert
  And over the sea.

One in a ship
  With a silver mast;
The fishermen wondered
  As he went past.

One on a horse
  With a saddle of gold;
The children came running
  To behold.

One came walking
  Over the sand,
With a casket of treasure
  Held in his hand.

All the people
  Said `Where go they?'
But the kings went forward
  All through the day.

Night came on
  As those kings went by;
They shone like the gleaming
  Stars in the sky.

Charles Williams

35

Holidays

Loading of our caravan,
Lifting, dragging, carting,
Holidays, dear holidays.
Starting,
        starting,
                starting.

Weather forecast: fine and cool.
Salty winds are blowing.
Not a word or thought of school.
We're going,
        going,
                GOING!

Carnivals along the coast,
Deck chairs, coloured brollies,
Marmalade and morning toast,
Fish and chips and lollies.

Where our bounding sea dog goes,
Where the netter dabs,
Pincering the tips of toes. . .
Irritated crabs.

Bring a bucket and a spade.
Hardly time to stop,
Bands upon the promenade,
Radios and Pop.

Trips around the tossing bay.
Climbing, leaping, chasing,
How the hours will fly away
Racing,
        racing,
                racing.

Back along the motorways,
Caravans are wending.
Holidays, dear holidays.
Ending,
        ending,
                ending.

Max Fatchen

Ghost story

You need a very good reader for this.
An adult who loves poetry could read it — and perhaps three children could act out the parts of Jack, Jim and Dan.
(Someone behind the scenes could sing in a 'small dry eggshell voice'.)

Bring out the tall tales now that we told
by the fire as the gaslight bubbled like a diver.
Ghost whooed like owls in the long nights
when I dared not look over my shoulder; animals
lurked in the cubbyhole under the stairs where the
gas meter ticked. And I remember that we went
singing carols once, when there wasn't the shaving
of a moon to light the flying streets. At the end
of a long road was a drive that led to a large
house, and we stumbled up the darkness of the drive
that night, each one of us afraid, each one holding
a stone in his hand in case, and all of us too brave
to say a word. The wind through the trees
made noises as of old and unpleasant and maybe
webfooted men wheezing in caves. We reached
the black bulk of the house.
'What shall we give them? Hark the Herald?'
'No,' Jack said, 'Good King Wenceslas.
I'll count three.'

One, two, three, and we began to sing,
our voices high and seemingly distant in the
snow-felted darkness round the house that
was occupied by nobody we knew. We stood
close together, near the dark door.
`Good King Wenceslas looked out
On the Feast of Stephen. . .'
And then a small, dry voice, like the voice
of someone who has not spoken for a long time,
joined our singing: a small dry eggshell voice
from the other side of the door: a small dry voice
through the keyhole. And when we stopped running
we were outside *our* house: the front room was lovely:
balloons floated under the hot-water-bottle-gulping gas;
everything was good again and shone over the town.

`Perhaps it was a ghost,' Jim said.
`Perhaps it was trolls,' Dan said,
who was always reading.

`Let's go in and see if there's any jelly left,'
Jack said. And we did that.

From *A Child's Christmas in Wales* by Dylan Thomas

38

A song for anyone to sing

There was a pig went out to dig,
On Chrisimas Day, Chrisimas Day,
There was a pig went out to dig
On Chrisimas Day in the morning.

There was a cow went out to plough,
On Chrisimas Day, Chrisimas Day.
There was a cow went out to plough
On Chrisimas Day in the morning.

There was a doe went out to hoe,
On Chrisimas Day, Chrisimas Day,
There was a doe went out to hoe
On Chrisimas Day in the morning.

There was a drake went out to rake,
On Chrisimas Day, Chrisimas Day,
There was a drake went out to rake
On Chrisimas Day in the morning.

There was a sparrow went out to harrow,
On Chrisimas Day, Chrisimas Day,
There was a sparrow went out to harrow
On Chrisimas Day in the morning.

There was a minnow went out to winnow,
On Chrisimas Day, Chrisimas Day,
There was a minnow went out to winnow
On Chrisimas Day in the morning.

There was a sheep went out to reap,
On Chrisimas Day, Chrisimas Day,
There was a sheep went out to reap
On Chrisimas Day in the morning.

There was a crow went out to sow,
On Chrisimas Day, Chrisimas Day,
There was a crow went out to sow
On Chrisimas Day in the morning.

There was a row went out to mow,
On Chrisimas Day, Chrisimas Day,
There was a row went out to mow
On Chrisimas Day in the morning.

Anon.

You can act this song out.

You'll need eight people (but you could have sixteen, if you changed the words to `There were TWO pigs went out to dig'. . .)

There's no need for fancy dressing up.

Pig — just pin a curly pink tail on behind. Needs a shovel.

Cow — two horns strapped to head. Needs a plough — use an old lawnmower, real or toy.

Doe — needs a hoe.

Drake — make a big bill. Needs a rake.

Sparrow — pin a few feathers here and there. Needs a harrow — use a chair tipped up with a broom tied underneath or think of something better yourself.

Minnow — pin a few fins on. Use a flour-sifter for a winnower.
Sheep — cottonwool pinned in a few places. A large pair of shears or scissors would do for reaping.

Crow — black cloak or paper draped round body. Sows a packet of seeds (use sand or small stones).

All actors join in the last verse.

You could do it like `The Twelve Days of Christmas'; after each line you repeat the one which went before, so that at the end you would say/sing:

There was a row went out to mow,
There was a crow went out to sow,
There was a sheep went out to reap,
There was a minnow went out to winnow,
There was a sparrow went out to harrow,
There was a drake went out to rake,
There was a doe went out to hoe,
There was a cow went out to plough,
There was a pig went out to dig,
On Chrisimas Day in the morning.

How far to Bethlehem?

How far is it to Bethlehem?
Not very far.
Shall we find the stable-room
Lit by a star?

Can we see the little child,
Is He within?
If we lift the wooden latch
May we go in?

May we stroke the creatures there,
Ox, ass and sheep?
May we peep like them and see
Jesus asleep?

If we touch His tiny hand
Will He awake?
Will He know we've come so far
Just for His sake?

Great kings have precious gifts,
And we have naught;
Little smiles and little tears
Are all we brought.

For all weary children
Mary must weep.
Here on His bed of straw
Sleep, children, sleep.

God in His mother's arms,
Babes in the byre
Sleep as they sleep who find
Their heart's desire.

Frances Chesterton

This could be read by someone with a
clear voice while a group hums an
appropriate carol very softly. The tune
of `Long Long Ago' fits in well; as does
`Away in a Manger'. Experiment with
different carols.

The Rabbit's Christmas Carol

I'm sick as a parrot,
I've lost me carrot,
I couldn't care less if it's
Christmas Day.

I'm sick as a parrot,
I've lost me carrot,
So get us a lettuce
Or. . .go away!

Kit Wright

Christmas Wreaths for the Door

1 Make a circle shape using wire, cane or vines. (You could use a coat hanger if you want a smaller wreath.)

2 Twist leaves, vines or grasses around your circle.

3 Add decorations such as pine cones, dried or fresh leaves, dried flowers, berries, seeds, grasses, herbs, pods, macaroni — even lollies! Attach these to your wreath using thin wire (such as fuse wire).

4 Finish it off with a bright red bow!

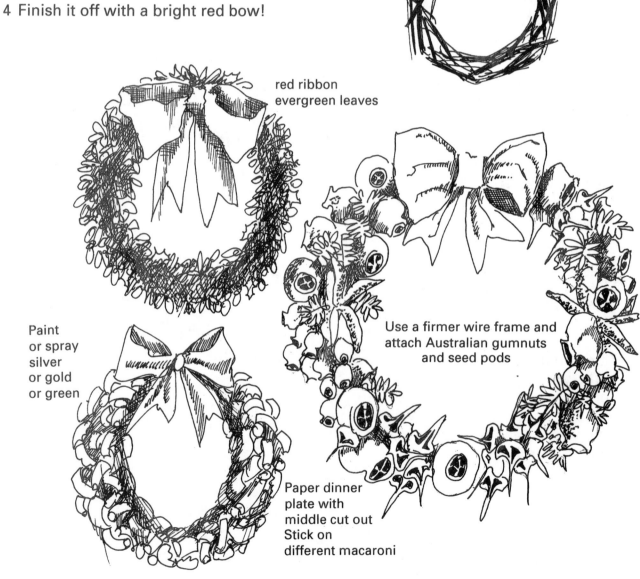

red ribbon
evergreen leaves

Paint
or spray
silver
or gold
or green

Use a firmer wire frame and attach Australian gumnuts and seed pods

Paper dinner plate with middle cut out Stick on different macaroni

Crumpled Wrapping Paper

1 Wet a sheet of paper (under tap, in a dish). Press on to an old newspaper to get rid of excess water.

2 Crumple the paper into a ball. Scrunch it up properly.

3 Carefully unfold. Place on an old newspaper.

4 Using a wide, soft paintbrush (or a pastry brush) paint the whole surface with watery poster paint.

Note: Use dark-coloured paints. Pale ones don't work!

5 Hold the painted paper under a tap. Most of the paint will wash off, but some will be left in the creases, giving this effect.

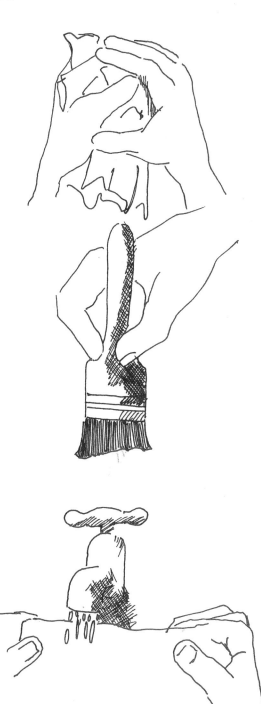

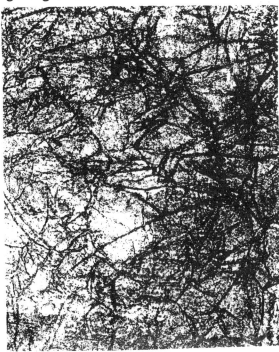

6 Be careful as the wet paper rips easily. Place the sheet on newspaper to dry.

Decorating a Christmas Parachute

You will need:

> an ordinary tissue or for an extra-special parachute, a large handkerchief
> some string
> sticky tape

1 Lay the tissue flat on the table and use the words and symbols in the box below to trace decorations for the parachute. Colour in with a felt-tipped marker.

2 Stick a small piece of sticky tape in each corner of the tissue. Make a small hole through the sticky tape in each corner.

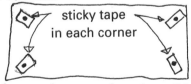

sticky tape in each corner

small hole in each corner

3 Cut four pieces of string 30-40 cm long.
Tie a piece of string to each corner.

4 Tie all the strings about 8cms from the bottom.

5 Tie the ends of the string to a small stone wrapped in a piece of foil or attach a matchbox with something light inside, to the strings.

6 Drop it from a height or throw it up into the air and watch it float.

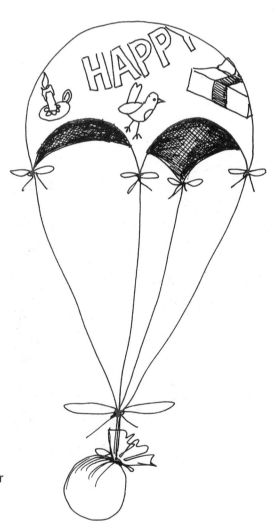

Decorative Pillows

These are just right for the family room!

You will need two pieces of material, each one about as big as a pillowslip — in fact, an old pillow slip would be fine.

You also need pins, cotton thread, wool, needles, scissors and pillow stuffing (pantyhose, material scraps, foam pieces).

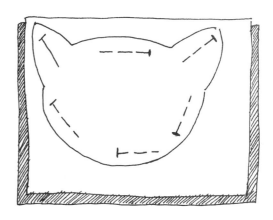

1 Take a large sheet of paper, decide on your pillow's size and shape, and outline your pattern.

2 Cut out the pattern and place it on the two pieces of material.
   Pin in place.
   Cut around the shape and unpin.

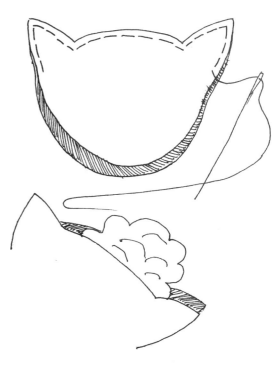

3 Sew the two pieces of material together, leaving a gap of 8-10cm for turning inside out and for stuffing.

4 Turn pillow inside out.
   (You might like to iron it.)

5 Decorate with felt pens, dyeing pastels or crayons. If you have made an animal, you could sew on a pink felt tongue, some buttons or sequins for eyes, and some string or woolly whiskers.

6 Stuff the pillow with old pantyhose, scraps of material or polystyrene pieces.

7 Tuck in the raw edges and sew the opening.

F

Flowers and Pots

A living present of flowers growing in a pot is always welcome. You can decorate a pot for another great gift idea.

Flowers

For *next* Christmas, start thinking NOW of plants you could grow in pots and give away.

If you DO happen to have a pot plant at home, wrap it up like this. It looks terrific!

1 Choose a large square of paper for wrapping your pot plant. (Green is best.)

Outline a square right in the middle of the square a little larger than the base of the pot plant.

2 Draw lines from the corners of the square to the edge as shown.

3 Cut away the shaded part.

4 Fold each of the four points up from the dotted line up to the top of the plant.

5 Make a hole through each point and tie together.

6 Tie with a bright red ribbon.
Let parts of the plant peep out from the sides.

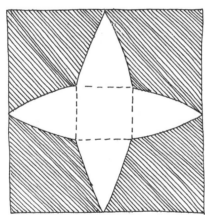

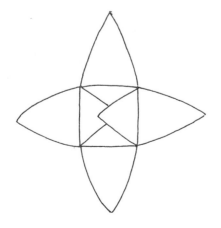

46

Pots

1 You will need an ordinary crock flower pot a bit bigger than your pot plant, a paintbrush, paint and clear varnish or Estapol.

2 Scrub the pot in hot water and detergent to remove grease from the surface which is to be painted.

3 Plan a design for the pot and sketch onto the surface with a soft pencil.

4 Decorate with acrylic or poster paint. Allow to dry thoroughly.

5 Apply varnish.

Flying Angel

You will need:
  blue or white felt
  silver fabric or white felt
  pink felt
  red felt

1 Look carefully at the pattern of the angel.

2 Using scissors cut out the body and arm shapes from the blue or white felt.
Cut out two of these shapes.

3 Cut out the face, hand and foot from pink felt.
Cut two of these.

4 Cut the wings from silver fabric or white felt.
Cut two of these.

5 Cut out same shapes from cardboard.

6 Stick felt shapes to both sides of the matching cardboard shapes.

7 Attach some ribbon and hang on Christmas tree.

Folded Cards

Cut-out cards

1 Fold a sheet of paper in half.

2 Draw a design on the right-hand side.

3 Cut around the design. Make sure you cut both layers.

4 Open out. Trim if there are jagged bits.

5 Decorate the outside. Write your message inside.

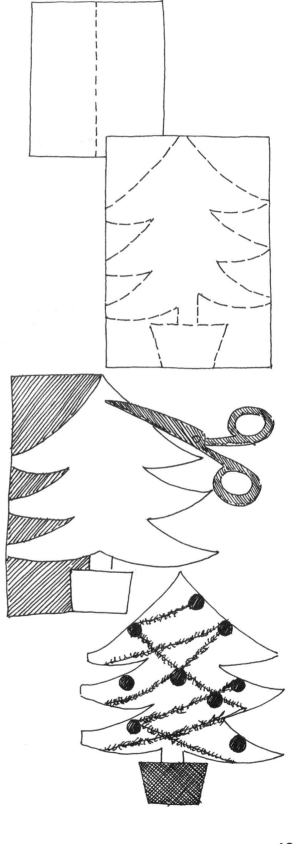

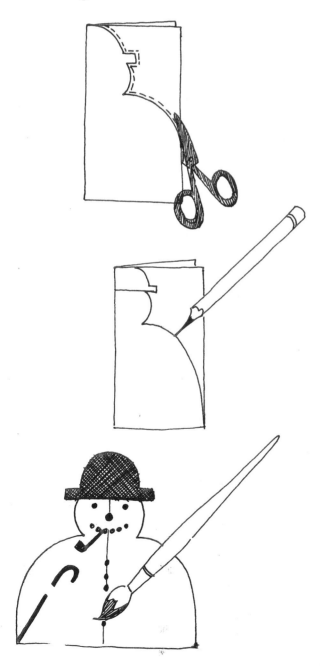

49

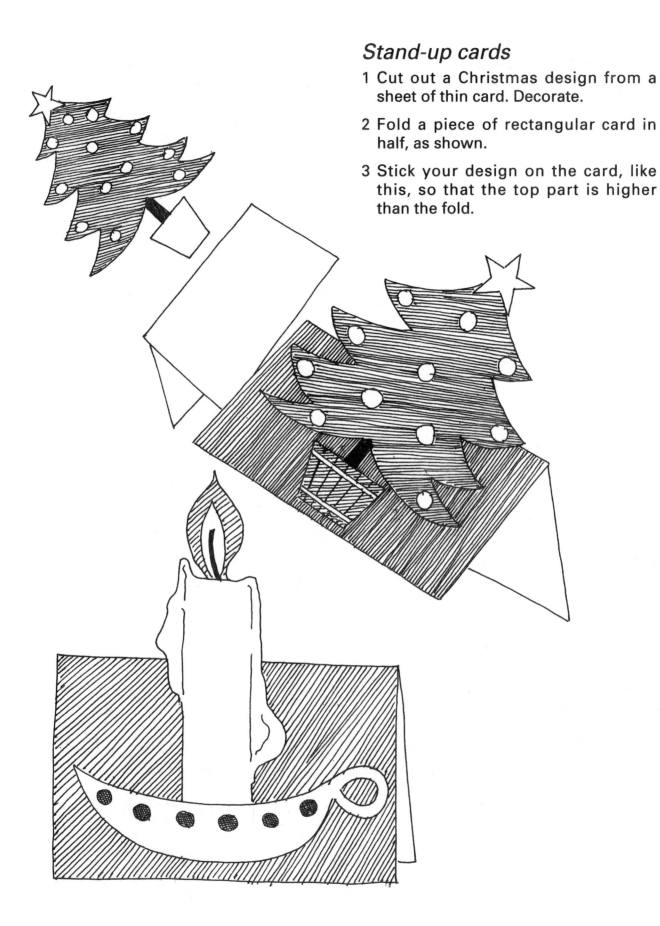

Stand-up cards

1 Cut out a Christmas design from a sheet of thin card. Decorate.

2 Fold a piece of rectangular card in half, as shown.

3 Stick your design on the card, like this, so that the top part is higher than the fold.

Folded Paper with Food Dye Dips

1 You will need some thin, absorbent paper for this. Kitchen roll tissue will do at a pinch, but smoother paper is better. A tissue hanky is too soft.

2 Fold a rectangle of this paper into a fan shape. (The width should be about two or three cms).

3 Put food dye or coloured inks into containers.

4 Now make your fan in this way.

Fold the end of the strip to the top edge.
Then fold the triangle part behind. (You take the strip back to the left.)
Fold the new end down to the bottom edge again, 'and fold the triangle back.
Keep on doing this until you get to the end. Your folded strip will look like this.

5 Fold your strip together as tightly as possible.

6 Dip one corner into the food colour and take it out very quickly — (almost straight away)!.

7 Now dip the other two corners in the food dye.
Take out quickly.

8 Let paper dry for ten minutes.

9 Unfold.
You should have an interesting pattern.

Note: Don't worry if you go wrong with the folding. This was a badly folded sheet, but look what happened!

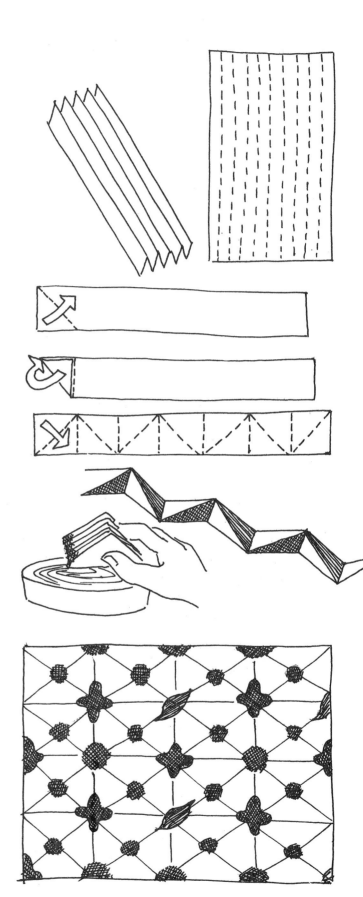

G

Games

Ball in a cone

1 Fold three sheets of newspaper together as shown to make the cone.

2 Roll the paper into a cone shape, tape edge in place.

3 Trim top so cone is about 30cm long.

4 Strengthen top edge with tape.

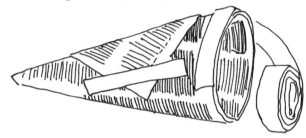

5 Draw two circles on a piece of firm material to make ball. Cut out.

6 Sew circles together, leaving an opening for stuffing.

7 Turn ball inside out and fill with rags, foam, etc. Tuck in the raw edges and sew.

8 Staple or sew a length of string (about a metre) to the ball. Staple other end of string to bottom of the cone (it goes inside, staple from outside).

9 To play, toss ball in the air and try to catch in the cone using one hand only.

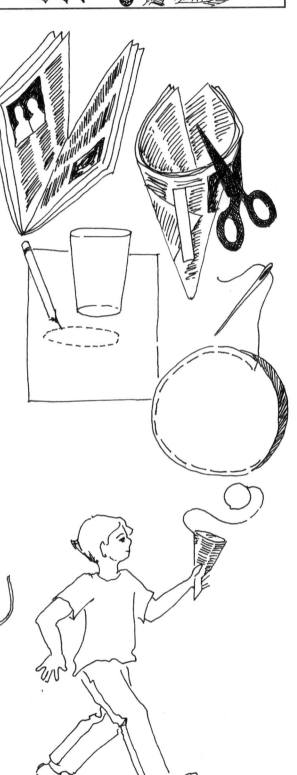

Hot cockles

Children used to play this game hundreds of years ago. One player is blindfolded and lies in the middle of the room.

The other players walk around him/her.

Every now and then someone gently touches the blindfolded person and calls out "Hot Cockles!"

Disguise your voice — make it sound quite different because the blindfolded person has to guess who has called out and touched them.

If they *do* guess correctly, that person must change places, and put the blindfold on.

Guess the carol

The leader taps the rhythm of a well-known Christmas song or carol. The person who guesses is the new leader.

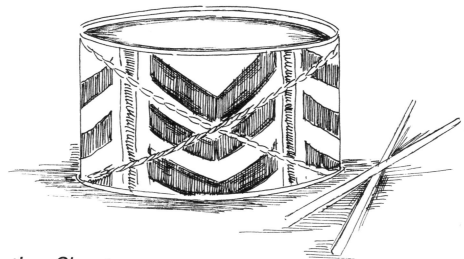

Santa's Action Chant

An adult leader reads the words	*The players make the actions*
Santa Claus stopped and paused,	Children stop and pause
He gave two sighs and rolled his eyes,	Sigh twice and roll eyes.
'It aches,' he said, as he rubbed his head.	Children rub heads, and keep on rolling eyes and sighing.
'I'd love some rum!' And he patted his tum.	Pat tums, keep on rubbing heads, rolling eyes and sighing.
He tapped one shoe — and we did too!	Tap shoes, while continuing all previous actions.
'Christmas is over,' he sleepily said. 'And now it's time to go to bed.'	Children cease all actions and 'sleep' on the floor. Shhhhh.

Christmas cacophony

Think of a title of a Christmas carol, book or song, e.g. 'The Night Before Christmas'.

Four players are chosen, one for each word:

Player 1 — The
Player 2 — Night
Player 3 — Before
Player 4 — Christmas

When the leader calls GO! each player must say his or her word at exactly the same time.

It is better if the leader takes the players outside the room beforehand for a quick whispered rehearsal. (It takes a bit of practice to get the words spoken at exactly the same time.)

Back inside, the group repeats the title over and over until the individual words are finally guessed or heard.

The first player to say the complete title is the leader of the next team.

Pin the star on the Christmas tree

This is a variation of Pin the Tail on the Donkey. Draw and colour a large Christmas tree on a sheet of paper.

Make a star to go on the top.

Pin the Christmas tree to a wall.

Each player is whizzed around a few times, and then has to pin the star to the top of the tree. (Eyes must be shut or a blindfold may be used.)

You could use other ideas for this game: Pin the antlers to the reindeer, or put the parcel in Santa's sack.

Christmas crickets

Make some small cardboard strips, about this big.

Fold them in half. When you press down they should s-p-r-i-n-g up.

(They should be about the same size (perhaps a bit bigger) as your finger nail.)

Make six crickets for each player. Use different colours for each player.

Trace the plan of the garden from the next page.

Take it in turns to spring the crickets into the garden from the edge of a table. Add up scores. The highest number wins.

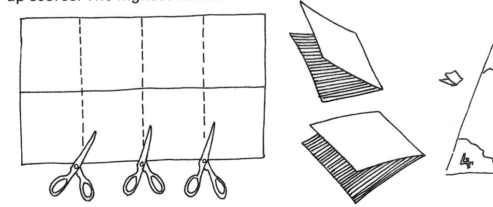

3 Flower beds

4 Santa arrives

6 Christmas tree

5 Pond

1 House

2 Lawn

Santa's helpers

Santa's helpers are frantic. It is nearly Christmas Eve and there is still so much work to do.

The Boss of the Helpers races in.

  (Use a large room, such as a hall or gym, for this game or a marked court.)

Leader or Boss says this	Other players do this
'Watch out for the reindeer! They're stampeding THIS WAY!'	All players rush in the opposite direction.
'Now they're coming THIS way!'	All players rush in the opposite direction.
'Now THIS WAY!'	As before.
'Now THAT way!'	As before.

The leader keeps on pointing in different directions and as soon as the players rush away, he or she calls out another direction VERY QUICKLY.

  This is usually a noisy game, with many loud shrieks. When things become too noisy, call out loudly,

- 'Down, DOWN — they're taking off!'.
  Players must lie on the floor AT ONCE to avoid the swiftly flying hooves!

Actions may be varied. Try some like this:

- Here comes Santa. All stand still. SMILE. Look busy.

  - Polish a toy truck.

  - Paint a toy farmyard.

  - Make yourself into a walking doll.

  - Make yourself into a tower of blocks.

  - Hammer some nails into a large model.

Gods' Eyes

In some countries, people believe that these gods' eyes will protect them from all harm.

1 You will need two twigs or sticks and some different coloured wools. (Twigs look much better than rulers or icy pole sticks.)

2 Make your twigs into a cross. Tie them together with fuse wire or string, like this:

3 Loop the wool around one arm of your cross.

4 Keep going around and around in the same direction.
Loop — around — NEXT ARM
Loop — around — NEXT ARM
and so on.
Make sure the wool is kept fairly tight.

5 Push each finished row in towards the centre. (If you run out of wool, just tie some more on. Put the knot at the back.)

6 Keep on going until you reach the edge of the cross. Fasten off.

7 Hang up. (Or wrap, to give away as a present.)

If you wanted to give a really good present of protection, you could make a mobile of different-sized gods' eyes.

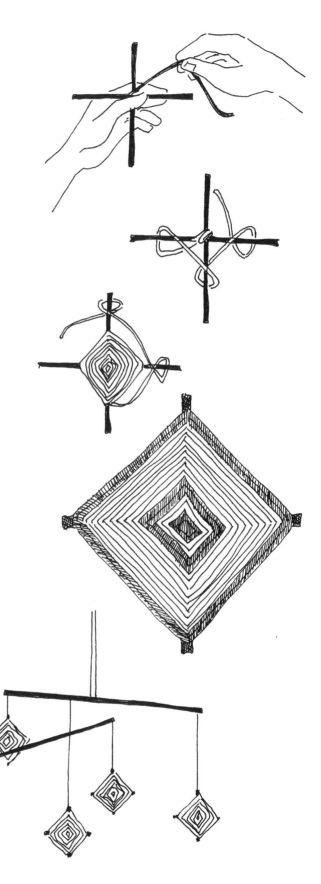

Great Sleigh Robbery

Note: to actors and teachers

- Remember, you don't have to follow the words of a play exactly. If you can think of better or funnier ideas, use them.

- For a list of props needed for this play, turn to the end of the play

CAST
Narrator
Father Christmas
Mother Christmas
Robber — Lefty
Robber — Muggsie
Robber — Al
Robber — Brain
Robber — Cruncher
Mother
Father
Girl
Boy
Grandma
Grandpa
Children (for Act 2) *Use the rest of the class and perhaps some keen people from other classes to give extra numbers.*

ACT I
(Spotlight on Narrator — stage left in front of curtain.)

Narrator   `Twas the night before Christmas,
When all through the house
Not a creature was stirring
Not even a mouse;
The stockings were hung
By the chimney with care
In hopes that St Nicholas
Soon would be there.
The children were nestled
All snug in their beds,
While visions of sugar-plums
Danced in their heads. . .

(pause)

Well, that's the way it was supposed to be. But this Christmas was different.

(Curtain opens — full lights to stage and Santa's workshop.)

(Enter Santa with Mother Christmas.)

Santa	Now, let's see. Have I got everything packed? Two thousand jet-hoppers?
Mother Christmas	Yes. (Ticking a list.)
Santa	1,127 rockets?
Mother Christmas	Yes. (Ticking a list.)
Santa	Three thousand skateboards?
Mother Christmas	Yes. (ticking a list.)
Santa	591 remote controls?
Mother Christmas	Yes. (Ticking a list.)

(Santa and Mother Christmas move to stage left with spotlight. Stage lights go off.)

Santa	Oh dear, oh dear. This is always a hard one.
Mother Christmas	What's wrong, dear?
Santa	Just look! Another request from some children Down Under. Every year I get someone asking for these. What can I do? (Spotlight on stage right, front.)
Song	`All I Want for Christmas is My Two Front Teeth'

(Full stage lights.)

Mother Christmas	Don't fuss. It's quite all right. Here are some surprise gifts that will make them forget all about their teeth.
Santa	Oh good! Well, I'd better get going. Don't forget to switch on my electric blanket. I'll be home at six.
(louder)	Now Dasher! Now Dancer! Now Prancer and Vixen! On Comet! On Cupid! On Donner and Blitzen! Ho! Ho! Ho! Ho!

(Curtain closes. Spotlight on Narrator.)

Narrator   Meanwhile, on top of the tallest building in the city, the most successful robbers in the world planned their greatest robbery.

(Spotlight from curtain right.)

Lefty   Muggsie, I'm sick of small-time jobs.
Let's do somethin' big.

Muggsie   Yeah, Lefty! Let's rob the Easter Bunny!
Just think of all that chocolate!

Al   Just think of all those pimples!
Anyway he's hardly started production yet.
What about Fort Knox, the greatest storehouse of gold in the world?

Brain   No, Al, No! Go for the BIG one. Let's hit the biggest flying toy supermarket in the universe — Santa's sleigh.
Just think — we'll be rich!

Lefty   But how can we do that, Brain?

Brain   Listen carefully. We'll all dress up as Santa Claus and hijack his sleigh by helicopter. Then we'll make off with the toys and dump Santa in the sea. We'll be rich beyond our wildest dreams. Let's get ready. Where's that box of disguises?

Al   Here it is, Brain!

Lefty   *(Holding up the large, bushy, black false moustache.)* This will do for Santa's beard, won't it boys? (He holds or sticks on moustache).

All Robbers   Yes! Good one! Beaudy! Rah! (etc.)

Muggsie   *(Holding up a pair of fancy slippers,)* And these will be just the thing for Santa's boots! *(He puts 'boots' on.)*

Al   *(Holding up a gaudy beach shirt)* And this will be PERFECT for Santa's coat. It's got a bit of red on it. [He puts it on.]

Brain   *(Holding up the hat with lots of ribbons and flowers.)* Wow! Look at this. Isn't it just like Santa's cap? (He puts it on.)

Cruncher   *(Holding up the frilly sissy pyjama pants.)* And there couldn't be anything more appropriate than these pants for Santa. (He then puts them on.)

Muggsie   That's it! No one could tell us from the real thing.
Let's go.

(Lights fade, curtain closes.)

ACT 2

(Curtain opens. Santa and sleigh are moving across the landscape. The sound of a helicopter is heard and becomes louder and louder.)

Santa   Holy candy bar! What's that?
The Eye-witness News Team is a bit too close for comfort tonight.

(Stage lights go off. Helicopter noise is really loud.)

Santa   Help! Help!

(Stage lights on dim.)

Cruncher   Just shut up, Santa, and get into the chopper. We'll take care of the toys, and as for the reindeer, you can forget about them. Their antlers will make wonderful hatracks for someone's wall. Ha! Ha! Ha! Ha!

(All robbers laugh.)

(Curtain closes. Spotlight on Narrator.)

Narrator   But the robbers had made one mistake. They had forgotten that at Christmas time children lie awake listening for sleigh bells and watching for a glimpse of Santa Claus. And so millions of children saw what happened. Dressing quickly they ran from their homes — and as fast as lightning the word of the kidnapping spread all over the world.

(Curtain opens. Spotlights on the robbers and Santa centre rear.)

Brain   OK. Head south for the hide-out and we'll split the loot. Make it fast!

Lefty   Coming in for a landing! Hey! What are all those kids doing down there? They're shouting and pointing! There's no way I can put down here.

(Stage lights on.)

(Scene — children come on shaking their fists at the robbers and shouting, `Let Santa go! Let Santa go! repeatedly.)

(Light on robbers and Santa.)

Al   Maybe this wasn't such a good idea!

Santa   It certainly wasn't!

Cruncher   Shut up, fuzzface, or you'll be chop suey when we get on the deck!

Lefty   Oh no! Oh no! We can't land here either! Look at those millions of kids. What can we do?

(Stage lights on.)

(Scene — children shaking their fists at the robbers.)

Brain   Mexico! Mexico! That's the place to go! All good crooks run to Mexico! Fly east to Mexico!

(Light on robbers and Santa.)

Muggsie   Yeah! The weather suits me better there, anyway!

(Stage light full on.)

Lefty   It's going to be tough landing here too. Look at all those creepy kids!

(Light on robbers and Santa.)

Cruncher   Kids, kids, wherever we go! What a shame we didn't bring a few fire hoses! Ha! Ha!

Santa   Oh dear, Christmas is supposed to be a time of peace.

Lefty   This is hopeless. We will have to give up. There's nowhere for us to land.

Brain   *(Untying Santa.)* Yes. But we'll have our revenge, Mr Claus. There'll be another chance next year.

Santa   Don't worry about that. There are thousands of disappointed kids everywhere. They've been waiting for me for hours. You've made me late delivering their presents. Now you MUST help me make up for lost time.

Muggsie   He's right. We've got no choice.

(Curtain closes, spotlight on Narrator.)

Narrator   So back they flew — over the North Pole, across the cities, deserts, jungles, oceans and mountains, still with angry shouts ringing in their ears. But all along the way Santa stopped the helicopter, and the grumbling robbers, laden with presents, slid — rather reluctantly — down the chimneys.

(Cruncher enters front right, children enter front left.)

(Lights on front stage.)

Girl   Hi, Santa! I knew you'd come! I've been waiting up for ages. Would you like some cake?

Boy   Have a nice hot cup of Milo. You must be really worn-out. What's the matter, Santa? Why are you shivering? And you look awfully thin this year. Have you been to Jenny Craig?

Cruncher   (Not quite so grumpy.)

Thanks, kids. Hey, this job is not so bad! Mmmm, this Milo's good — nearly as good as rum! I might have to give up stealing.

(Boy, girl, Cruncher exit.)
(Curtain opens, stage lights on.)

Brain	Listen, Mr Claus, I'm enjoying this job. Any chance of some full-time work?
Cruncher	Yes, Mr Claus. We'd all like to help.
Santa	Ho, Ho, Ho! Call me Santa, boys. Of course you can work for me.
Narrator	In fact the great sleigh robbers are still with Santa. They hate the weather, but they love the work. They especially like inventing new toys — perhaps they've made one of your favourites.

And most of all they enjoy Christmas Eve when they help Santa to load up the sleigh and deliver toys to children all over the world. |

Props

For this play you will need the following Props (a theatre word meaning properties).

ACT 1

Santa's workshop

1 Lots of different sized boxes with TOYS written in large letters (on the side facing the audience).

Pile toys all over the boxes and floor. (Ask everyone in your class to bring old toys from home.)

2 A table with a large sign which reads: THE TALLEST BUILDING IN THE WORLD

3 A large box marked DISGUISES It must contain:

- a large, bushy, black false moustache

- a pair of fancy slippers or pink, ballet-shoes with ribbons

- a gaudy beach coat or shirt

- a hat with lots of ribbons and flowers

- some frilly sissy pyjama pants.

ACT 2

Helicopter noises

A tape or a person making helicopter noises is needed right at the beginning of the act. (A person would be funnier. Record the class comedien and turn the tape up full volume!)

Santa and sleigh

Use your imagination. An upside down table with reins would be O.K. Use moving lights or sounds to give the impression of movement. Or try something else. (Kids often have great ideas!)

Adapted from the picture book *The Great Sleigh Robbery.*

Jars, Bottles and Boxes

Jars and bottles

1 Collect interesting jars and bottles.
2 Decorate by sticking on labels, stars, strips, buttons, braid, sequins — anything you fancy!
3 Leave jars or bottles empty for Mum to fill with special things or fill with lollies, bath salts or tiny soaps.

Boxes

Cover a box with dried seeds, flowers, grasses (or shells). Use PVA or superglue. This box could be used to hold special possessions of a friend or relation. Or you could cover a box with buttons and label it.

Magical Christmas box

1 Measure up this shape on a large piece of card.
2 Trace in the dotted lines, then cut out the shape.
3 Score along the dotted lines. (This means to press firmly with the non-cutting edge of a pair of scissors.)
4 Fold the shape into a box.
5 Copy the pictures from the borders of this page. Colour them in and use them to decorate your Christmas box.

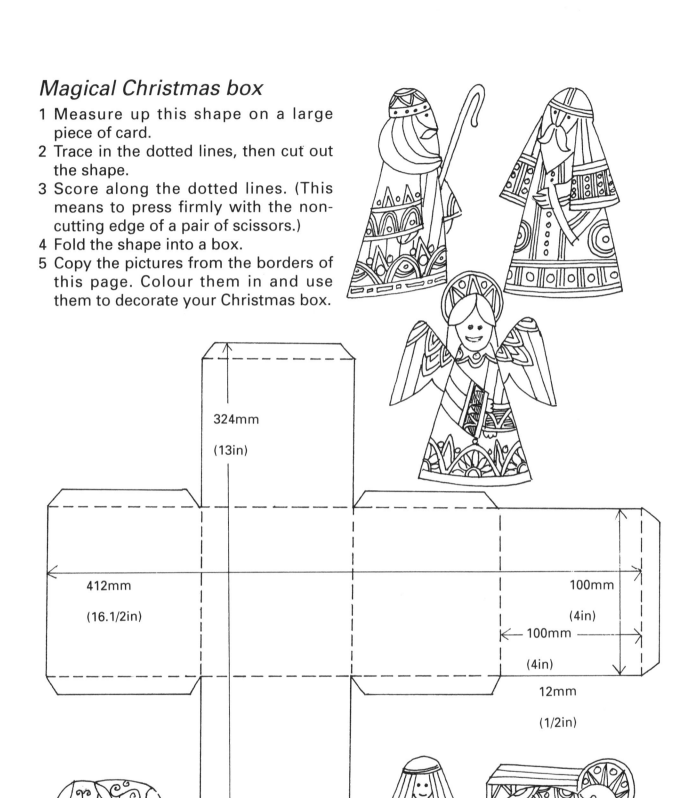

324mm

(13in)

412mm

(16.1/2in)

100mm

(4in)

100mm

(4in)

12mm

(1/2in)

Miniature Christmas box

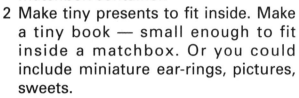

1 Make a matchbox into a tiny present
 container that nobody could resist.
 You could use threads or tinsel,
 sequins, tiny edge of sequins, stars,
 cottons, beads to decorate your
 matchbox container.
2 Make tiny presents to fit inside. Make
 a tiny book — small enough to fit
 inside a matchbox. Or you could
 include miniature ear-rings, pictures,
 sweets.
3 Make a tiny card to go with the
 present.

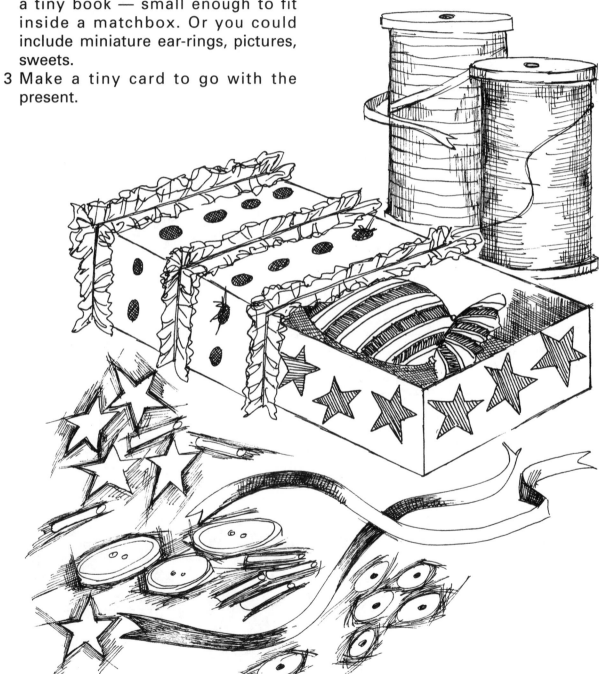

Jigsaw Puzzle

1 Cut out the Christmas scene — along the dotted line.

2 Stick the scene on firm card.

3 Use brightly coloured marker pens or textas to colour in the scene.

4 Carefully work out where you want to cut the picture.

5 Cut it up.

6 Mix the pieces and see if you can do your own jigsaw.

7 To make a second jigsaw, draw your own scene and follow numbers 1-6.

Kindergarten Christmas Play Rehearsal

You will need:

> A frazzled teacher
> Four little children (the STAR)
> Joseph
> Mary
> Innkeeper
> Good reader
> A loud crying voice
> Other carol singers

(Four large pieces of cardboard, marked with the letters S, T, A, R (one letter to each piece),

Scene: Part of a rehearsal for the kindergarten's Christmas play

`A few carol singers straggle on stage and stand in a huddle. They begin to sing:
Silent night, (Loud bang!! followed by an OUCH!)
Holy night (It was YOUR fault! It was NOT!)
All is calm, all is bright (The first verse continues while loud whispers, bangs and thumps go on in the background.)

When the first verse is over, the teacher rushes on stage.

Teacher   Hurry up, shepherds. Start singing verse two, carol singers.

Carol singers   (Sing.) They looked up and saw a star

Teacher   (loud whisper —) AGAIN, please, singers
They looked up and saw a star
and saw a star
and saw a star
and saw a star

(This sounds like a cracked old record)

Teacher   (Urgently.) SHEPHERDS!! Hurry! STAR people! Hurry!

The shepherds straggle on. Four little STAR people each holding up a letter come on stage. They don't know what to do.

Teacher (loudly whispering) Spread out, spread out. (The four little STAR people look at each other, bewildered. Finally they stand apart, holding their letters up.)

(They read:)

Teacher No, no. Simon, you swap places with Yvette, and Anna . . .

They change places:

Teacher No, swap again . . .

(This time, the letters read:)

(They look puzzled as the audience laughs.)

Teacher Let's try the scene at the inn. Where's the innkeeper?

Voice He's away today.

Teacher Would someone volunteer, please?

(One of the little RATS volunteers.)

Reader So Joseph and Mary were desperate for somewhere to sleep. It was dark and cold, and they had travelled a long way.

Joseph Here's an inn. (He knocks.) Could my wife and I stay here the night, please?

Innkeeper Um, um . . .

Teacher
(whispering loudly.) Say `There's no room at the inn!'

Innkeeper There's no room at the inn.
(Mary begins to cry. Joseph comforts her.)

Innkeeper
(Going over to Mary.) Don't cry, Tracey, please don't cry. You can have MY room. I'll sleep outside.

Teacher   Let's get this over quickly.

We'll finish with `Away in a Manger'.

All the actors sing `Away in a Manger' beautifully.

When it comes to the line

`But Little Lord Jesus no crying he makes'

the baby in the manger begins crying loudly, then more loudly and finally SO VERY LOUDLY that he drowns out the singing and the curtain falls.

(The crying could be made by someone behind the curtain or someone hiding behind the manger.)

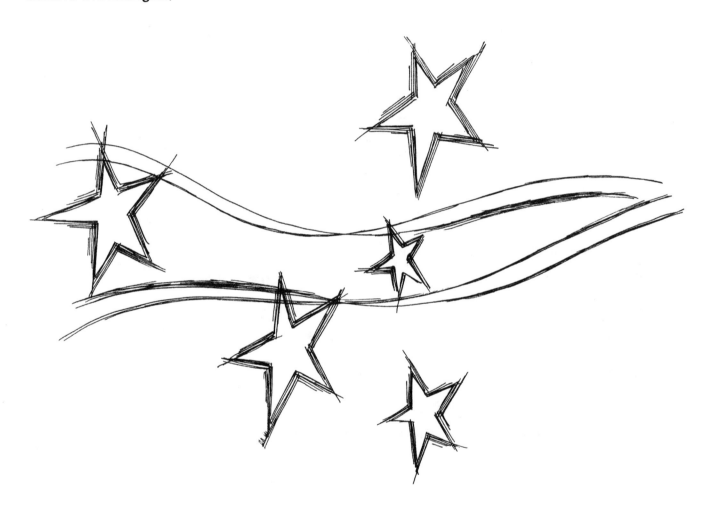

Lanterns

Simple strip lantern

1 Fold paper in half lengthways and cut as shown. (Use Christmas wrapping paper for a different effect).

2 Unfold paper.

3 Stick the sides together with glue, tape or staples.

4 Attach a handle to the top. Use paper, wool, pipe-cleaners or a strip of paper.

You can make tiny lanterns to decorate the Christmas tree or larger ones to decorate the room.

See-through strip lantern

1 Fold and cut paper as for the previous lantern, but this time cut out every second strip.

2 Open up paper.

3 Stick the edges together.

4 Your lantern will be a similar shape to the previous one, but there is a space between each panel.

5 Attach a handle and hang up.

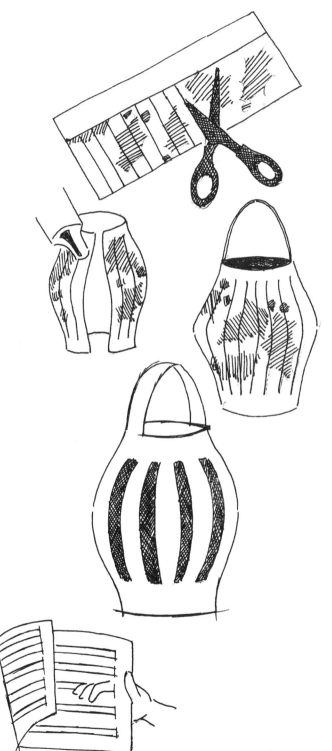

cut-out
shaded parts

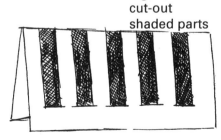

Lolly Paper Parcels

You will need some lollies wrapped in coloured paper.

1 Use a plain paper (even newspaper would do!) to wrap a parcel.

2 Wrap a ribbon round the parcel.

3 Tie a piece of very thin ribbon or fuse wire to each lolly like this.

4 Attach to ribbon on the parcel. No one will notice the dull paper!

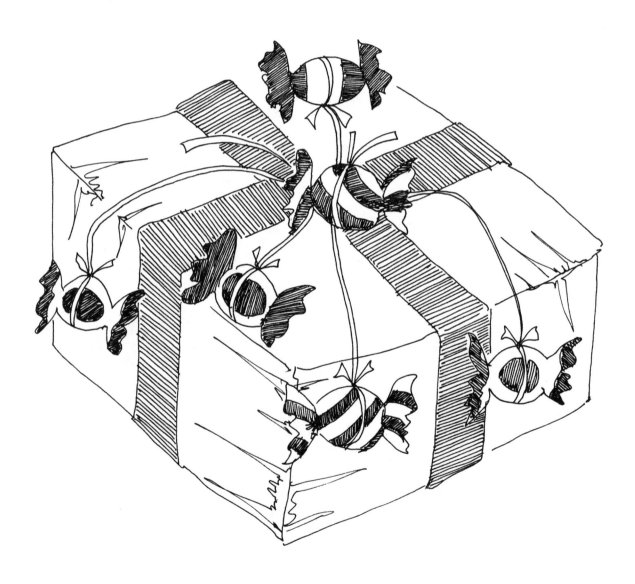

Mimes

Cut these mimes out and stick onto a sheet of thin card or firmer paper.

Shuffle the cards, and keep them in place with a rubber band.

One person takes a card from the stack, reads it secretly and then acts out what is written.

The person who guesses correctly has the next turn. (You could do some of these mimes as part of a concert or other entertainment. The audience would enjoy joining in!)

- You are unwrapping an enormous parcel. You tear the paper off expectantly. It reveals a very heavy book: How To Study Harder.

- You are a parent sneaking into your child's bedroom to place the presents at the foot of the bed.

- You wake up on Christmas morning to find there are no presents anywhere!

- You are the Christmas star.

- You see three ships come sailing by.

- You are pulling a cracker with a friend.

- You blow up a balloon until it is so huge you are sure it will burst. It does!

- You are opening an exciting box. It is empty.

- You are saying the grace before Christmas dinner.

- You are not able to get to sleep on Christmas Eve.

- You are Santa — stuck in the chimney!

- You are trying to clean up the mountain of wrapping paper torn off the whole family's presents.

- Your Gran is watching as you open her present. It is a pair of socks!

- You hear a knock on the door on Christmas Eve. It is your little brother playing a trick.

- You are one of Santa's helpers carrying an enormous sack of toys.

- You are a walking doll.

- You are taking a photo of your baby sister under the tree.

- You are chasing the dog away from the tree and the presents.

- You are pretending to sing `Silent Night, Holy Night'.

- Your Christmas candle will not light.

- You are watching Carols by Candlelight when you see your face on the huge TV screen.

- You are wrapping a very large and awkwardly shaped parcel.

- You are walking back from the shops, laden with parcels and bags. You cross a road, but drop everything! Cars toot. You pick them up — and drop them again!

- You are one of the Three Wise Men

walking into the stable with gifts for Baby Jesus.

- You are one of the shepherds guarding over the sheep when the Angel of the Lord appears. You are terrified.

- You are Joseph, pleading with the innkeeper to allow Mary and you to stay for the night.

- You are the innkeeper telling Joseph that there is no room at the inn.

- You are the angel on the Christmas tree.

- You hang some mistletoe above the door and then stand under it, hoping that someone will kiss you.

- You are the Christmas tree.

- You are a neatly wrapped parcel with a bow.

- You are Santa trying to land with his sleigh and his reindeer on a very windy roof.

- You eat so much Christmas dinner that you can hardly walk away from the table.

- You swallow a coin from the Christmas pudding, but someone pats you on the back and it comes up. You are relieved!

- You are playing 'Silent Night' on the piano.

- You are making a Christmas card for a friend.

- You are trying to carry an armful of holly but it keeps prickling you.

- You are a bell-ringer on Christmas Day.

- You are listening to Christmas bells. They are so loud that you are nearly deafened.

- You make a sandcastle in the shape of a snowman.

- You are making the longest paper chain in the world.

- You are trying to make a pair of wings for an angel in the play.

- You are decorating the Christmas tree.

- Santa invites you to ride in his sleigh.

- Santa's helper in a large city store is exhausted at the end of a long sticky day. He finds it hard to keep smiling at little children.

- The chimney is full of soot so Santa gives up and comes in the front door.

- A little child is trying to tie a bow for a parcel.

- You are stirring the Christmas pudding.

- You are wishing on a star.

- You are riding your Christmas rocking horse.

- You are building a very high tower with your Christmas blocks.

- At last! You approach the calendar and cross off 23 December. It is Christmas Eve!

Note: You could colour the simpler mimes a different colour to make it easier for younger children.
Or you could whisper a simple mime and then let them act it.

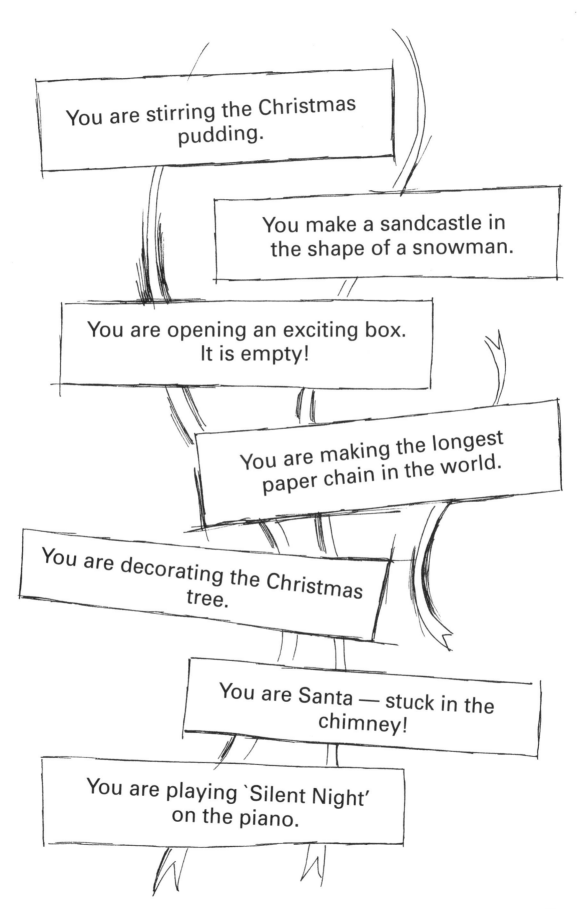

You are stirring the Christmas pudding.

You make a sandcastle in the shape of a snowman.

You are opening an exciting box. It is empty!

You are making the longest paper chain in the world.

You are decorating the Christmas tree.

You are Santa — stuck in the chimney!

You are playing 'Silent Night' on the piano.

Mobiles

Any of the small tree ornaments described could be used to make simple mobiles.

Find a coathanger and dangle some of the decorations at different lengths.

(Cover the coathanger with tinsel or crepe paper first, if you like.)

Mouth-watering Christmas Party Food

Chocolate fruits

You will need:

> 250g mixed glace fruits
> 125g dark chocolate

1 Chop fruit into bite-size pieces; place in bowl.

2 Put chopped chocolate in top of a double saucepan.

3 Stir over simmering water until chocolate has melted (Don't let the water touch the bottom of the saucepan otherwise the chocolate might overheat).

4 Remove pan from heat.

5 Place a piece of fruit on end of skewer, dip into chocolate, gently tap skewer against side of saucepan to drain off excess chocolate.

6 Use another skewer to push chocolate coated fruit onto foil.

7 Refrigerate until chocolate is firm.

Christmas trifle

You will need:

> 1 jam-filled swiss roll
> 2/3 cup orange juice
> 1/4 cup lemon juice
> 2 tablespoons extra fruit juice
> 470g can sliced peaches
> 1 pkt port wine jelly crystals
> 470g can pineapple pieces
> 6 passionfruit
> 1 punnet strawberries

Custard

> 2 cups milk
> 2 tablespoons custard powder
> 2 tablespoons sugar
> 1 teaspoon vanilla

1 Make jelly as directed on packet. Refrigerate until set.

2 Wash and hull strawberries. Soak in extra fruit juice.

3 Cut swiss roll into lcm rounds; arrange evenly over base of a big bowl.

4 Combine orange juice and lemon juice; mix well.

5 Spoon mixed orange and lemon juice over swiss roll slices.

6 Arrange drained peaches on top of swiss roll.

7 Pour over half the cold custard.

8 Spoon chopped jelly on top of custard.

9 Then put drained pineapple and passionfruit pulp over jelly.

10 Pour over remaining custard.

11 Decorate with whipped cream and strawberries.

To make custard

1 Blend custard powder with a little of the milk.

2 Now add remaining milk and mix well.

3 Stir in sugar.

4 Stir over low heat until mixture boils and thickens.

5 Remove from heat. Allow to cool.

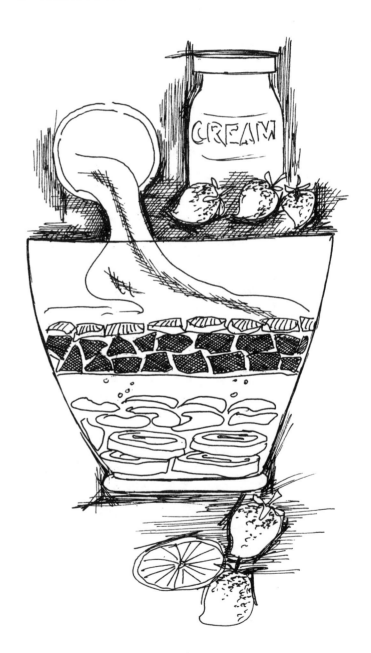

Gingerbread men

You will need:

225g plain flour
pinch of salt
2 teaspoons ground ginger
150g butter
1 egg separated
2 tablespoons black treacle
25g sugar plus 15g sugar to glaze
a few currants for decoration
icing sugar and food colouring
(optional)

1 Sift the flour, salt and ground ginger into a bowl.

2 Rub in the butter until the mixture resembles fine breadcrumbs.

3 Add the egg yolk, black treacle and sugar and mix thoroughly.

4 Knead lightly and roll out on a floured surface to 5mm thick.

5 Cut out gingerbread men shapes and place on greased baking tray.

6 Brush with egg white, sprinkle with sugar, and decorate with currants.

7 Bake in moderate oven, 180C, for 12-15 minutes.

8 Cool slightly on the baking tray then move to a wire rack.

9 Decorate with icing.

Note: It might be fun to decorate the gingerbread men to make Father Christmas biscuits by adding red icing hats and white icing beards.

Christmas pudding trick

You will need:

bucket
wallpaper paste and water
silver or gold foil
paper plate
newspaper torn into strips
a plastic bowl turned upside down
vaseline
gum nuts
gum leaves
brown and white paint and varnish

1 Make the paste. Empty the contents of the packet into a bucket of water. Stir until it's like a jelly that's a bit runny.

2 Tear a sheet of newspaper into strips like this.

3 Put vaseline on the upturned bowl.

4 Dip the strips of paper into the paste and paste these strips of paper over the surface of the upturned bowl.

5 Leave this to dry for a couple of days.

6 When dry carefully lift the pudding shape from the bowl.

7 Paint the pudding shape with brown paint.

8 Dribble white paint over the top to look like custard sauce. When it's dry cover with varnish.

9 Decorate the paper plate with foil.

10 Paint the gum nuts in Christmas colours.

11 Put the pudding on the plate and top with gum nuts and leaves.

Too good to eat! How many people were tricked?

Santa cake

You will need:

    3 cake mixes, your favourite
    1 round cake tin
    2 square cake tins

1 Bake cakes according to instructions on packet.

2 When cakes are cool cut into pieces following this pattern.

3 Cover a large piece of cardboard or chipboard with foil.

4 Arrange Santa Claus on the board.

5 Ice Santa with red, pink, black and white icing where appropriate.

6 Use sweets such as licorice, marshmallows, raspberries, for decoration for eyes, beard, buttons, etc.

7 Enjoy eating it!

Nativity Play or Pageant

You will need:

> Carol singers
> Mary (carrying a doll), Joseph
> Shepherds (any number)
> Angels
> Three Kings
> Manger, straw, costumes

Actors in a pageant do not speak any words, but everyone should know all the words of the carols to be sung. See pages 16 to 33 for the music for these carols.

Carol singers are at the back of the stage.

All other actors are backstage, waiting for their turn. (All people — even those back stage — sing while they are waiting.)

O Little Town of Bethlehem

1 O little town of Bethlehem,
   How still we see thee lie!
   Above thy deep and dreamless sleep
   The silent stars go by.
   Yet in thy dark streets shineth
   The everlasting light;
   The hopes and fears of all the years
   Are met in thee tonight.

2 For Christ is born of Mary
   And gathered all above,
   While mortals sleep, the angels keep
   Their watch of wond'ring love.
   O morning stars, together,
   Proclaim the holy Birth,
   And praises sing to God our King,
   And peace to men on earth.

While this is sung, Joseph and Mary come on stage and enter stable.

Away In A Manger

1 Away in a manger, no crib for a bed,
   The little Lord Jesus lay down His sweet head.
   The stars in the bright sky look'd down where He lay,
   The little Lord Jesus, asleep in the hay.

2 The cattle are lowing, the Baby awakes;
   The little Lord Jesus, no crying He makes
   I love Thee, Lord Jesus, look down from the sky,
   And stay by my cradle till morning is nigh.

Mary and Joseph move a little to the left as `Away in a Manger' is finished, and the next carol begins.

The First Noel

1 The first Noel the angel did say
   Was to certain poor shepherds in fields as they lay
   In fields where they lay keeping their sheep
   On a cold winter's night that was so deep
   Noel, Noel, Noel, Noel,
   Born is the King of Israel.

2 They looked up and saw a star
   Shining in the East beyond them far,
   And to the earth it gave forth great light,

And so it continued both day and
    night.
Noel, Noel, Noel, Noel,
Born is the King of Israel.

3 Then let us all with one accord
   Sing praises to our Heavenly Lord,
   Who hath made heaven and earth of
     naught,
   And with His blood, mankind hath
     bought.
   Noel, Noel, Noel, Noel,
   Born is the King of Israel.

**The shepherds come on stage at
the beginning of this carol, and at
the right place in the carol, the
angels appear.**

Hark! The Herald Angels Sing

1 Hark! the herald angels sing
   Glory to the new-born King!
   Peace on earth and mercy mild,
   God and sinners reconciled.
   Joyful all ye nations, rise,
   Join the triumph of the skies,
   With the angelic host proclaim,
   Christ is born in Bethlehem.
   Hark! the herald angels sing,
   `Glory to the new-born King!'

2 Hail, the heav'n-born Prince of Peace,
   Hail, the Son of Righteousness;
   Light and life to all He brings,
   Ris'n with healing in His wings.
   Mild, He lays His glory by,
   Born that man no more may die;
   Born to raise the sons of earth,
   Born to give them second birth.
   Hark! the herald angels sing,
   `Glory to the new-born King!'

**The angels and shepherds move to
the back of the stage and join the
carol singers. The Three Kings
enter.**

We Three Kings

1 We three kings of Orient are;
   Bearing gifts we traverse afar
   Field and fountain, moor and
   mountain,
   Following yonder star:

Refrain

O, star of wonder, star of night,
Star with royal beauty bright,
Westward leading,
Still proceeding,
Guide us to thy perfect light.

Melchior:
2 Born a King on Bethlehem's plain,
   Gold I bring to crown Him again,
   King forever, ceasing never,
   Over all to reign.

Refrain

Caspar:
3 Frankincense to offer have I,
   Incense owns a Deity nigh,
   Pray'r and praising, all men raising,
   Worship Him, God most high.

Refrain

Balthazar:
4 Myrrh is mine, its bitter perfume,
   Breathes a life of gathering gloom;
   Sorrowing, sighing, bleeding,
    dying,
   Seal'd in the stone-cold tomb.

Refrain

All
5 Glorious now behold Him arise,
   King and God and Sacrifice,
   Alleluia, Alleluia,
   Earth to the heav'ns replies.

Refrain

**All the cast is now assembled on
stage, the Three Kings sing their
parts, and for the finale everyone —
audience included sings `Silent Night'.**

Silent Night

1 Silent night, holy night,
   All is calm, all is bright
   Round yon Virgin mother and
     child,
   Holy infant so tender and mild,
   Sleep in heavenly peace,
   Sleep in heavenly peace.

2 Silent night, holy night,
   Shepherds quake at the sight;
   Glories stream from heaven afar,
   Heav'nly hosts sing Alleluia;
   Christ the Saviour, is born,
   Christ, the Saviour, is born.

3 Silent night, holy night,
   Son of God, love's pure light
   Radiant beams from thy holy face,
   With the dawn of redeeming
     grace,
   Jesus, Lord, at thy birth,
   Jesus, Lord, at thy birth.

If you want your nativity play to have spoken words (as well as the carol singing) make up a short play basing it on the Christmas story in the Bible. You will need to add a few extra characters — such as the innkeeper and King Herod, if you decide to include him.

Carol Concert

If there are not enough people for a nativity play or pageant, you could organise a carol-singing concert. Make a booklet of words (see Christmas Carol Collection, page 16).
Some carols can be acted. You might like to try these.

Good King Wenceslas

Three people are needed — King Wenceslas, his page, the poor man trekking through the snow, plus extra singers.

1 Good King Wenceslas looked out
   On the Feast of Stephen,
   When the snow lay round about,
   Deep, and crisp, and even:
   Brightly shone the moon that night,
   Though the frost was cruel,
   When a poor man came in sight,
   Gath'ring winter fuel.

2 'Hither, page, and stand by me;
   If thou know'st it, telling,
   Yonder peasant, who is he,
   Where and what his dwelling?'
   'Sire, he lives a good league hence,
   Underneath the mountain,
   Right against the forest fence,
   By Saint Agnes' fountain.'

3 'Bring me flesh, and bring me wine,
   Bring me pine logs hither.
   Thou and I shall see him dine,
   When we bear them thither.'
   Page and monarch forth they went,
   Forth they went together;
   Through the rude wind's wild lament,
   And the bitter weather.

4 "Sire, the night is darker now
   And the wind blows stronger.
   Fails my heart, I know not how,
   I can go no longer'
   "Mark my footsteps my good page
   Tread thou in them boldly.

Thou shalt find the bitter wind
Freeze thy blood less coldly,

5 In his master's steps he trod
Where the snow lay dinted
Heat was in the very sod
Which the saint had printed.
Therefore Christian men be sure
Wealth of rank possessing;
Yes who now will bless the poor
Shall yourself find blessing.

The Twelve Days of Christmas

1 On the first day of Christmas
my true love sent to me,
a partridge in a pear tree.

2 On the second day of Christmas
my true love sent to me,
Two turtle doves,
and a partridge in a pear tree.

3 On the third day of Christmas
my true love sent to me;
three French hens, two turtle doves,
and a partridge in a pear tree.

4 On the fourth day of Christmas
my true love sent to me,
four calling birds, three French hens,
two turtle doves and a partridge in a
pear tree.

5 On the fifth day of Christmas
my true love sent to me,
five gold rings, four calling birds,
three French hens, two turtle doves,
and a partridge in a pear tree.

6 On the sixth day of Christmas
my true love sent to me,
six geese a-laying, five gold rings,
four calling birds, three French hens,
two turtle-doves, and a partridge in a
pear tree.

7 On the seventh day of Christmas
my true love sent to me,
sev'n swans a-swimming, six geese
a-laying,
five gold rings, four calling birds,
three French hens, two turtle doves,
and a partridge in a pear tree.

8 On the eighth day of Christmas
my true love sent to me,
eight maids a-milking, sev'n swans
a-swimming,
six geese a-laying, five gold rings,
four calling birds, three French hens,
two turtle doves, and a partridge in a
pear tree.

9 On the ninth day of Christmas
my true love sent to me,
nine ladies dancing, eight maids a-
milking,
sev'n swans a-swimming, six geese
a-laying,
five gold rings, four calling birds,
three French hens, two turtle doves,
and a partridge in a pear tree.

10 On the tenth day of Christmas,
my true love sent to me,
ten lords a-leaping, nine ladies
dancing,
eight maids a-milking, sev'n swans
a-swimming,
six geese a-laying, five gold rings,
four calling birds, three French hens,
two turtle doves, and a partridge in a
pear tree.

11 On the eleventh day of Christmas
my true love sent to me,
elev'n pipers piping, ten lords a-
leaping,
nine ladies dancing, eight maids a-
milking,
sev'n swans a-swimming, six geese
a-laying,
five gold rings, four calling birds,
three French hens, two turtle doves,
and a partridge in a pear tree.

12 On the twelfth day of Christmas,
my true love sent to me,
twelve drumers drumming,

elev'n pipers piping, ten lords a-
    leaping,
nine ladies dancing, eight maids a-
    milking,
sev'n swans a-swimming, six geese
    a-laying,
five gold rings, four calling birds,
three French hens, two turtle doves,
and a partridge in a pear tree.

This is a funny action song. It can be
very energetic — all those repeated
actions are vigorous — you really need
the first five lines to recover!

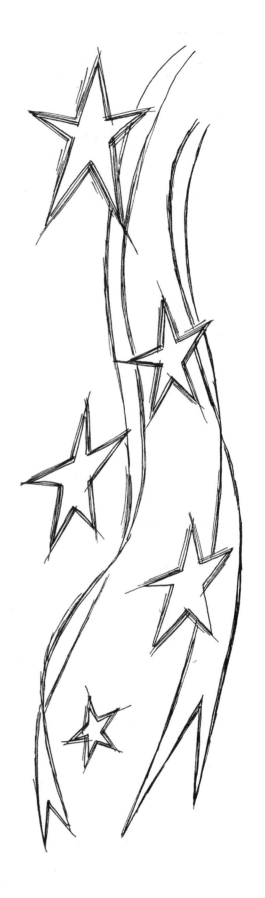

sing these five verses without actions	1	partridge in a pear tree
	2	turtle doves
	3	French hens
	4	calling birds
	5	gold rings
make the appropriate actions for every line	6	geese a-laying
	7	swans a-swimming
	8	maids a-milking
	9	ladies dancing
	10	lords a-leaping
	11	pipers piping
	12	drummers drumming

While Shepherds Watched and *We Three Kings* are two more acting carols.

Finish off the concert by singing *We Wish You A Merry Christmas.*

We Wish You a Merry Christmas.

We wish you a Merry Christmas!
We wish you a Merry Christmas!
We wish you a Merry Christmas
and a happy New Year!
Glad tidings we bring to you and your
    kin,
We wish you a Merry Christmas
and a happy New Year!

Costumes

Angels
Make tunics from white material (even an old sheet). Use lengths of tinsel for head and wrist bands and to cross over the front of costumes.

Shepherds
Make tunics from textured heavier material. Jerkins or furs can be worn. Use tea-towels as scarves or head-dresses. Shepherds carry a staff, a toy lamb or a lantern.

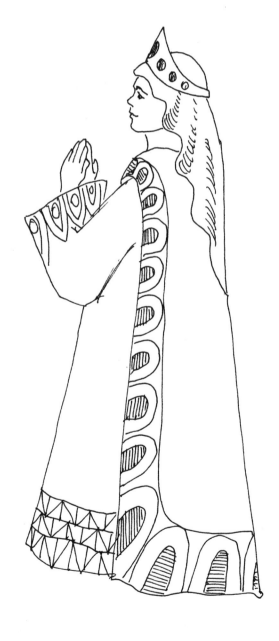

Innkeeper

Use richer fabric to make tunic. Tie cummerbund round waist. Add necklaces, bracelets or brooch.

Three Wise Men

Make tunics from luxurious fabric. A cloak may be worn, decorated with fur or jewels. Make crowns from cardboard, decorate with sequins, silver stars, etc. Alternatively a long scarf can be tied into a tall turban.

Nativity Scene to Make

The nativity scene always includes Mary and Joseph, and the baby Jesus in the crib. It may also have shepherds, the three wise men, an angel, and the animals standing about, all in the stable.

The following instructions will help you make a simple nativity scene.

The stable

You will need:

> large cardboard box — a minimum of 18cm in height
> paint
> shredded paper or dry grass
> corrugated cardboard
> tape or glue
> twigs
> plasticine
> pipecleaners
> tinsel

1 Paint your box inside and out in 'stable' colours.

2 Turn the box on its side (see diagram) and scatter finely shredded paper or dry grass on the floor for straw.

3 Make the roof by taking a sheet of corrugated cardboard a bit bigger than the box. Paint it to match the stable. Lay it flat on top or bond it to form a ridge. Secure the roof with tape or glue.

4 Stand a few small twigs against the wall of your stable. Secure their 'feet' with plasticine.

5 Use three or four pipe-cleaners to make a star for the roof. Twist them together to make a star shape. Add some tinsel to make it shine, then secure it firmly to the highest point of the roof.

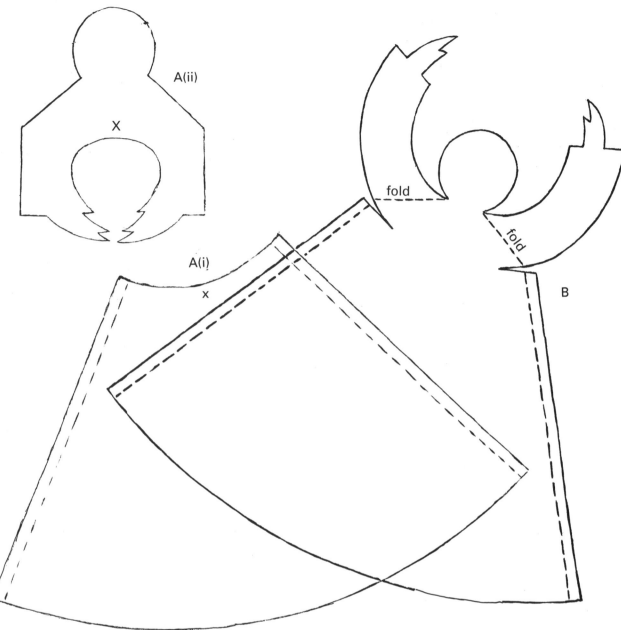

The figures

You will need:

  stiff paper or light card
  scissors
  paints, textas, or coloured pencils

1 Trace shapes A(1) and (ii), B, C, and C(1) and D(ii) onto stiff paper or light card.

2 Very lightly with pencil label the back of each shape with the correct name: A is for Joseph, B is for Mary, C is for the baby, D is for the crib.

3 Cut out the shapes.

4 Draw faces onto Mary, Joseph and the baby.

5 Colour their clothes, and the crib.

6 Shapes A, B and C. Join the cone-shaped pieces along the dotted lines. Secure with sticky tape or glue.

7 Join A(i) and A(ii) together at X, and secure with sticky tape. Fold the arms of B where shown. Join the hands in front of the body.

The Crib

You will need:

    tape
    baby doll to put into crib

1 Shape D. Snip the ends of D(ii) where they are marked.

2 Fold into a curve as illustrated.

3 Tape the two end pieces, D(i), into place to make the crib.

4 Place the baby in the crib.

5 Group the figures as shown, inside the stable.

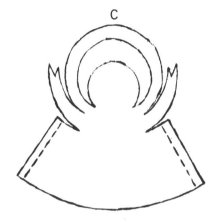

C

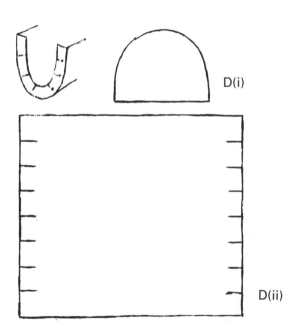

D(i)

D(ii)

Wise men, shepherd, angel

1 To make these use either figures A or B.

2 Dress the shepherd simply, like Joseph.

3 Dress the wise men in grand style. attach the decorative headdresses (cut out E and F), and sprinkle these and their clothes with glitter (add glue first so that the glitter sticks!)

4 For the angel, trace G. Apply glitter. Place the wings into the top of the cone behind the head.

To complete your nativity scene

1 Group the figures around the stable.

2 Place the angel at the back of the stable, behind the Holy family.

3 Add trees by using twigs or small branches secured in lumps of plasticine.

E

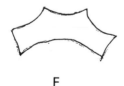

F

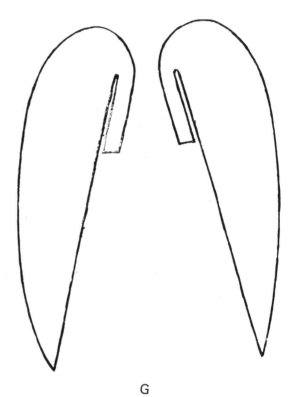

G

Old Favourite Games

Don't forget to play some old games.

Pass the parcel round the ring

Wrap a small present in dozens of sheets of paper. Pass it round. When the music stops (someone tapping a stick on the floor will do), the person holding the parcel takes off one sheet. Continue this process until the last sheet of paper is removed.

Dressing up for dinner

You need some old clothes in the centre of a circle and a block of chocolate. Throw a dice. When a player gets a 6 they must dress in the clothes and begin to eat the chocolate with a knife and fork. If another player throws a `6' before the other one has even had a mouthful of chocolate that's bad luck. Sometimes another `6' might be thrown before you've even put one arm in a coat! That's the way it goes!

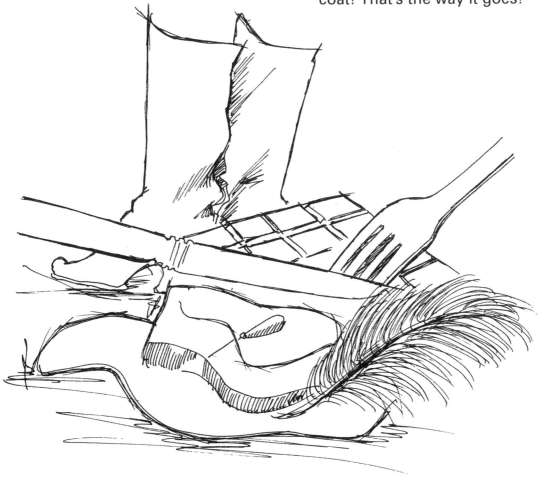

Origami Christmas

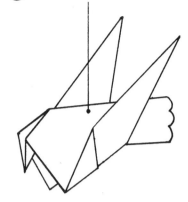

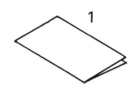

1

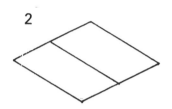

2

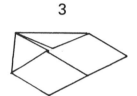

4

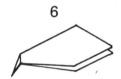

3

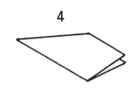

5

6

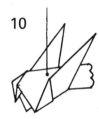

7

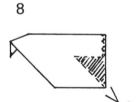

8

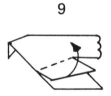

9

10

Christmas dove

You will need:

1 sheet of 15cm x 15cm paper

1 Fold paper in half into a rectangle.

2 Unfold.

3 Fold two corners into the centre.

4 Fold paper in half.

5 Fold head down to about 3-1/2cm from edge, creasing well.

6 Fold head backwards on the same crease, again creasing well.

7 Return head to original position, and push top down, reversing the middle crease.

8 Draw wing and tail, and cut away shaded part.

9 Fold wings up at slightly different angles so a bit of the other wing shows.

10 Hang with ribbon or string on the Christmas tree.

Christmas tree

You will need:
   1 sheet of 15cm x 15cm paper
   glue

1 Fold paper in half into a triangle.

2 Unfold.

3 Fold edges into centre line.

4 Fold edges into centre line.

5 Rotate paper 90° anticlockwise.

6 Divide line AB into four equal parts. Fold point B up to line 2.

7 Fold bottom edge up.

8 Fold trunk down.

9 Glue flaps, and turn tree over.

10 Colour tree with spray paint and decorate with tinsel and glitter.

11 Place tree on the party food table as a decoration.

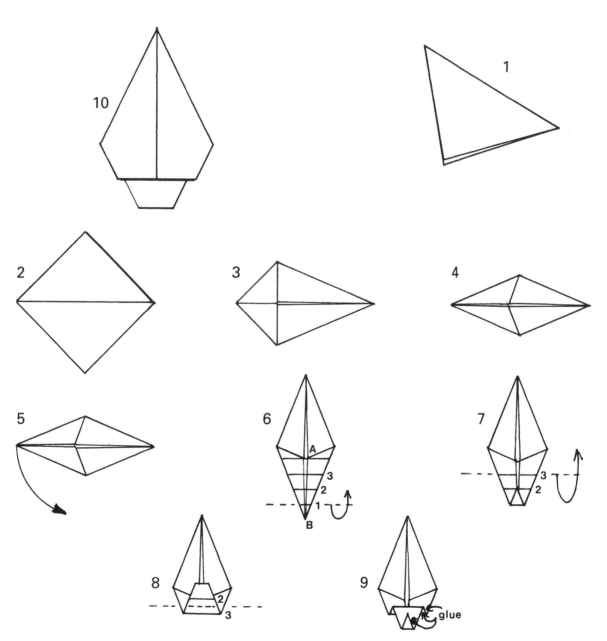

95

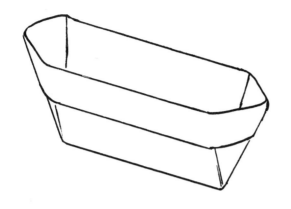

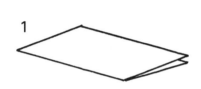

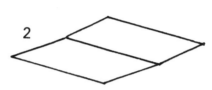

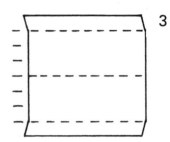

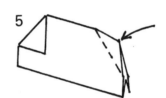

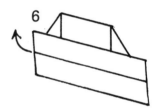

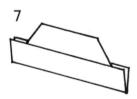

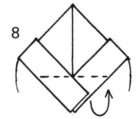

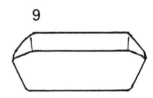

Manger

You will need:
 1 sheet of 15cm x 15cm paper

1 Fold paper in half into a rectangle, creasing well.

2 Unfold.

3 Fold edges one third of the way to the centre.

4 Fold paper in half into a rectangle.

5 Fold corners down like this.

6 Fold bottom edge up.

7 Turn paper over and repeat step 6.

8 Open bottom, overlapping ends and folding ends inside.

9 Add hay and a doll and use this in your nativity scene.

Ornaments

Stones

Collect interesting shaped stones, and paint them to represent various creatures.

Here's how you can make a different creature using more than one stone.

1 Choose a large stone for the body.

2 Add small stones for arms or legs. Cover small stones with PVA or superglue. Allow the glue to become sticky. Press firmly into place.

3 Paint or add other features.

Cones

1 Press a pine cone into a clay or plasticine base.

2 Add a seed-pod head, if you can find one, or cut from cardboard.

3 Stick on eyes and feet.
  Make up some creatures of your own. The mousey gumnut will start you off with ideas.

Paper Hats

Everyone has a favourite way of making party hats.

The easiest hats

1 Take a strip of coloured paper. Crepe paper is good because it stretches. Staple together to form a circular shape.
The paper must be long enough to fit a head — some adults have BIG heads and require about 60cm! Don't forget to allow an extra few centimetres for joining.

2 Cut out some Christmas shapes. Stick one onto each hat.

3 Glue or staple ends to form hat.

Zig-zag hats

1 Cut a strip of paper big enough to fit a head.

2 Cut out zig-zag shapes as shown.

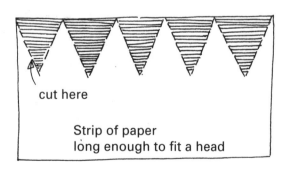

cut here

Strip of paper
long enough to fit a head

3 Colour or decorate.

4 Glue or staple ends to form hat.

Fringed hats

1 Cut a strip of paper 60cm x 18cm.

2 Cut halfway along the strips as shown.

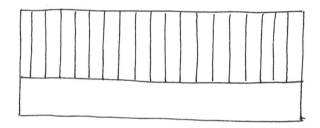

3 Curl along the cut edges as shown. You could cut each edge to make a fringe.

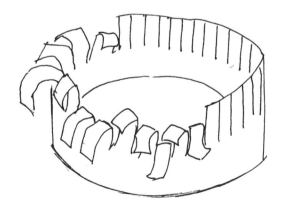

Circle hats

1 Trace around a plate (placed over a sheet of paper).
Cut out the circle.

2 Cut as shown.

3 Decorate with Christmas shapes.

4 Join up the edges with tape or staples.

5 If it's a small hat, you might need to tie it on!

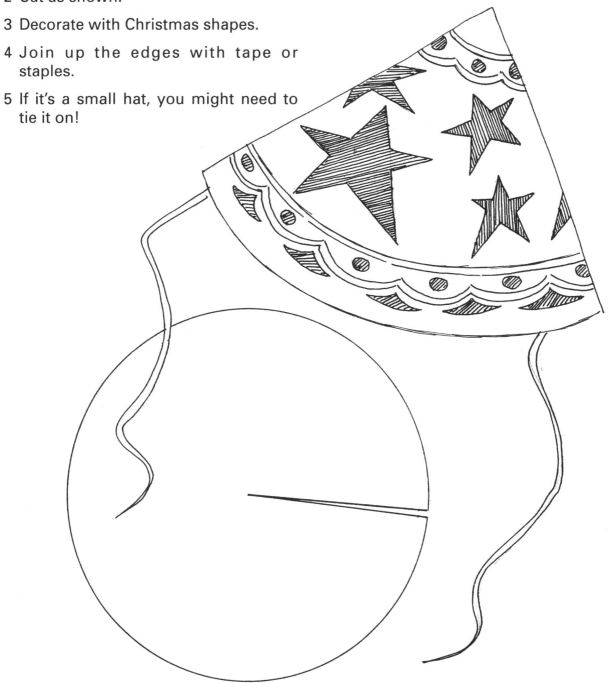

Patterns, Pictures and Borders

Use these to copy, trace, or as stencils
for your Christmas posters, cards,
letters and art work.

Place Cards

These show people where to sit at the table, and can be later kept as a souvenir of the Greatest Christmas Party Ever!

Simple fold-over cards

1 Fold a piece of paper (9cm x 10cm) horizontally.

2 Write the person's name on one side of the paper.

3 Colour in and decorate.

Folded card shapes

1 Fold a firmer piece of paper (9cm x 10cm) in half, vertically.

2 Cut out a Christmas shape.

3 Write the person's name on the card. Colour and decorate.

4 Stand the card on the table.

Placemats

Whether you're preparing a party for Christmas at home or at school, if you make the table look inviting and exciting by preparing beautiful decorations, the food will taste all the better.

Hand-drawn mats

1 Draw a Christmas scene on a sheet of firm paper or thin card (30cm x 26cm). Colour brightly.

2 Cover with see-through adhesive such as Fablon.

Woven mats

1 Fold a sheet of paper (30cm x 26cm) in half.
Make cuts as shown.

2 Open paper out.

3 Make about 15 strips of brightly coloured paper (2cm wide, 26cm long).
Or you could make 30 thinner strips (1cm wide) but this would take ages to do!

4 Use two contrasting strips of coloured paper and weave as shown.

5 Draw a Christmas border round the edges.

6 Stick to a firmer sheet of card.

7 Cover with adhesive.

Printed mats

Use any of the printing methods described on pages 107-109 to print your own placemats.

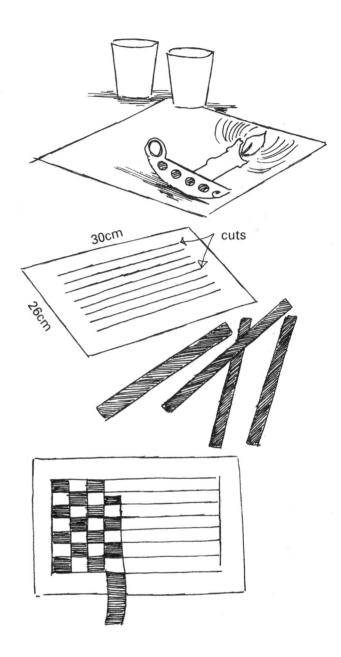

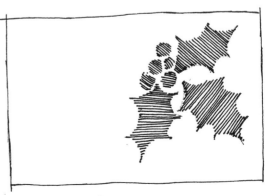

Poems and Pictures

Pictures

If you have done a picture or painting you're proud of, why not frame it and give it to a favourite relative for Christmas? Buy a frame or make one from cardboard or paper.

A book of poems

1 Fold some sheets of paper in half to form a book.

2 Select about six poems you really like and copy them out neatly on the pages. Write the name of the poet underneath each poem.
Then write a poem especially for the person who is to be given the book. Write YOUR name under this poem.

3 Illustrate the poems.

4 Think of a title for the collection. Make a cover and a title page. Don't forget the dedication!

5 Sew or staple your poems into a book.

These presents cost very little but we can promise you they will be treasured by the person you give them to.

Pop-up Cards

1 Trace this design onto a sheet of firm paper (or thin card).

2 Cut around the THICK BLACK lines. Use very sharp pointed scissors (or a Stanley knife, if an adult is helping). DO NOT CUT OUT COMPLETELY. Just cut along the thick lines.

3 Fold along the dotted lines.

4 Decorate.

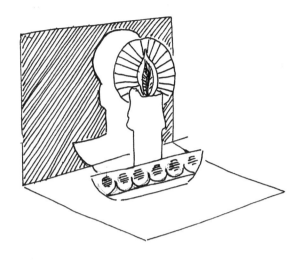

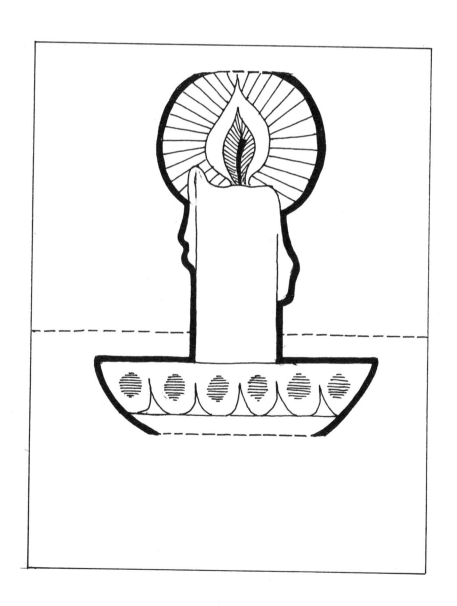

Printed Cards

Using the methods described in `Printed Paper' overleaf print your own Christmas cards. (You might like to make matching cards and wrapping paper.)

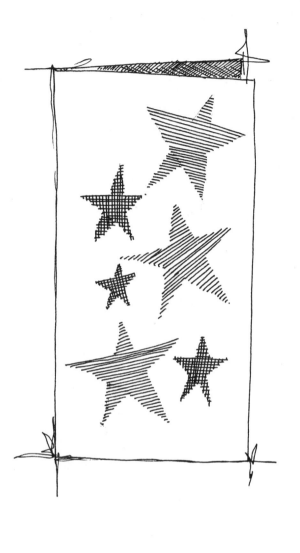

Printed Paper

Potato prints

1. Cut a potato in half, using a sharp knife. Cut it neatly.

2. Scratch a design on the inside with a knife tip. (Even small children can make simple designs such as stars.)

3. Cut the potato away like this so that your pattern or design stands out.

4. Put some paint in a container and press the potato into it.

   Note: We think it's better to paint your potato with a brush — not so much paint oozes and gushes!)

5. Press your painted potato design onto a sheet of scrap newspaper. (This is important.)
   Experiment to find out how much paint you'll need. If you use too much your design will be globby.

6. Now print onto the sheet of paper you wish to use.

7. Let it dry.

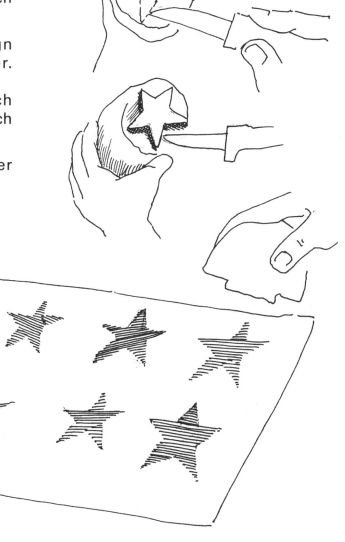

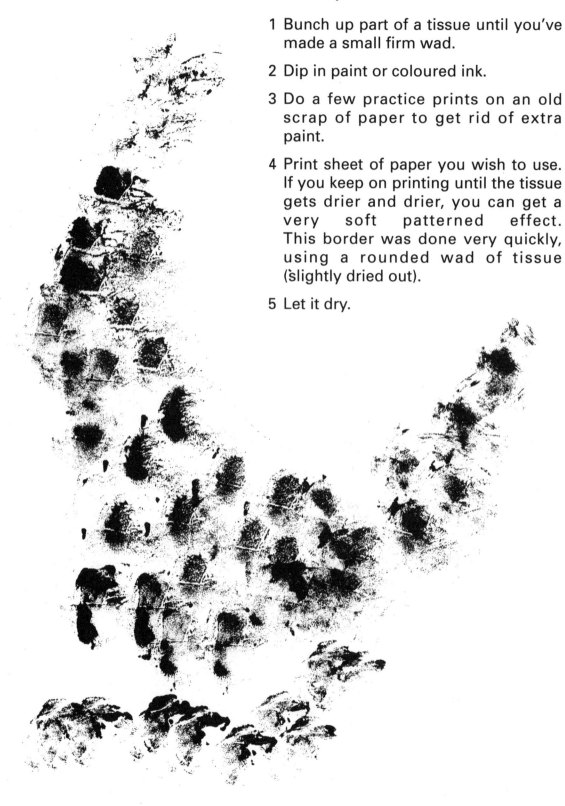

Tissue prints

1 Bunch up part of a tissue until you've made a small firm wad.

2 Dip in paint or coloured ink.

3 Do a few practice prints on an old scrap of paper to get rid of extra paint.

4 Print sheet of paper you wish to use. If you keep on printing until the tissue gets drier and drier, you can get a very soft patterned effect. This border was done very quickly, using a rounded wad of tissue (slightly dried out).

5 Let it dry.

Cotton bud prints

Dip buds in paint, food dye or inks to make a picture, pattern or border on your paper.

Sponge prints

1 Cut a kitchen sponge in half.

2 Roll it up tightly. Hold it firmly.

3 Paint one side of the longer part, using a paintbrush and poster paint.

4 Get rid of extra paint by pressing a few times onto an old piece of newspaper.

5 Press onto paper.

6 Or use the rolled up end.
   The sponge absorbs the paint so well that you can print many times before it runs dry.
   This is a quick and easy printing method.

Other prints

You can print using absolutely ANYTHING. . .(almost).
   Try a comb, buttons, leaves, cardboard tubes, lids of bottles. . .

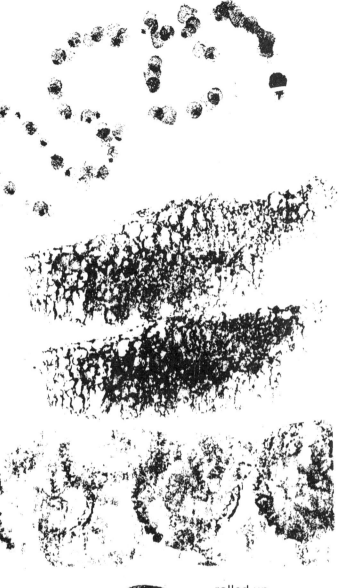

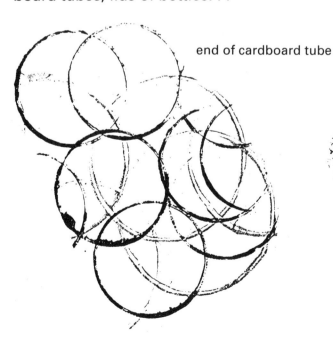

end of cardboard tube

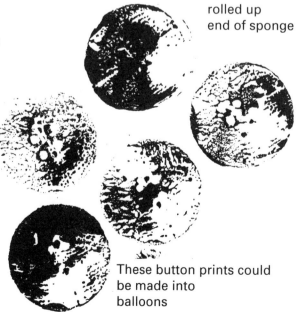

rolled up
end of sponge

These button prints could be made into balloons

109

Puzzles

Christmas carol word search

Find the Christmas carols in this word search. Like any word search, the answers can go across, backwards, upwards, downwards, or diagonally. Give a copy of this puzzle to a friend as a present.

K	F	V	M	S	R	A	L	I	C	O	X	S	N	P	E	V	O
C	H	R	I	S	T	M	A	S	D	A	Y	P	Y	U	S	O	N
K	C	O	M	E	A	L	L	Y	E	F	A	I	T	H	F	U	L
N	D	I	L	O	N	R	V	E	S	D	G	H	W	R	B	I	S
A	W	E	T	H	R	E	E	K	I	N	G	S	N	E	H	J	M
E	V	K	C	Z	W	F	E	R	G	U	S	E	M	G	D	U	E
R	P	K	I	K	N	S	H	Q	U	T	R	E	A	N	H	A	H
N	O	N	A	J	T	U	L	I	E	D	E	R	S	A	J	L	E
O	H	T	I	S	V	H	S	U	A	L	I	H	S	M	O	A	L
T	C	T	H	C	I	B	E	A	J	A	N	T	E	A	Y	N	H
H	H	E	I	E	R	G	I	H	N	I	A	W	P	N	T	E	T
G	R	F	E	F	F	R	L	I	A	C	I	A	T	I	O	Y	E
I	I	R	L	O	F	I	U	I	S	L	E	S	J	Y	T	A	B
N	S	M	E	S	C	E	R	L	A	I	L	I	R	A	H	E	F
Y	T	P	A	I	K	T	I	S	T	J	R	S	I	W	E	C	O
B	M	I	A	L	A	T	M	N	T	I	C	A	T	A	W	H	N
S	A	L	S	E	C	N	E	W	G	N	I	K	D	O	O	G	W
K	S	E	R	N	T	H	L	B	Y	G	O	E	E	N	R	I	O
C	T	I	N	T	S	I	T	A	T	L	I	W	N	G	L	O	T
O	R	V	R	N	F	M	T	L	T	E	B	E	E	R	D	W	E
L	E	E	R	I	O	H	E	U	A	B	L	F	O	L	M	H	L
F	E	M	H	G	N	W	A	L	Y	E	A	G	T	A	L	I	T
R	G	E	A	H	G	H	T	A	E	L	H	N	L	O	K	L	T
I	U	H	I	T	A	S	T	L	H	L	I	S	G	N	I	E	I
E	G	N	Y	L	R	E	L	O	A	S	P	L	O	T	S	S	L
H	T	D	E	H	C	T	A	W	S	D	R	E	H	P	E	H	O

These carols are hidden in the word search. . .

Away In A Manger; O Little Town of Bethlehem; While Shepherds Watched Their Flocks By Night; Silent Night; Balulalow; Christmas Day; We Three Kings; The First Nowell; Come All Ye Faithful; I Saw Three Ships; Deck The Halls; Joy To The World; Jingle Bells; Oh Christmas Tree; Good King Wenceslas.

Christmas picture crossword

So that you will know which clues you
have solved, colour in the pictures as
you find the answers.

Happy Christmas puzzle

Solve the puzzle across and read the message down.

A tree with prickly leaves
and red berries.   ☐ ☐ ☐ ☐ ☐

We sing them at Christmas   ☐ ☐ ☐ ☐ ☐ ☐

——— the Red Nosed Reindeer   ☐ ☐ ☐ ☐ ☐ ☐ ☐

—— Pudding   ☐ ☐ ☐ ☐

Silent Night, —— Night   ☐ ☐ ☐ ☐

Another name for Father
Christmas. Santa ——   ☐ ☐ ☐ ☐ ☐

The town where Jesus was born ☐ ☐ ☐ ☐ ☐ ☐ ☐ ☐ ☐

Baby Jesus was placed in
a ——— in a stable   ☐ ☐ ☐ ☐ ☐ ☐

There was no room at the
— for Mary and Joseph   ☐ ☐ ☐

He was a good king   ☐ ☐ ☐ ☐ ☐ ☐ ☐ ☐ ☐

You can be kissed under this ☐ ☐ ☐ ☐ ☐ ☐ ☐ ☐

One of the gifts brought
by the three wise men   ☐ ☐ ☐ ☐ ☐

Hark the Herald —— sing   ☐ ☐ ☐ ☐ ☐ ☐

An earlier kind of Father
Christmas. Saint ———   ☐ ☐ ☐ ☐ ☐ ☐ ☐ ☐

The crack-a-jack Christmas code play

Solve the puzzle, then rewrite it as a play and act it out.

The scene	Inside a Robber's Cave
The time	Christmas Eve
The characters	Three robbers: Dobber, Blobber, Clobber, (later)Lady Sweetness Fortes cue-Smythe-Browne (in this story the surname is usually abbreviated to F-S-B)

1

The three robbers sat in unhappy silence. They had no money, no food and no plans for a cheerful celebration. `This is going to be the worst Christmas we have ever had,' they moaned. `Wait! I have an idea,' said Blobber.'

2

`12.9.19.20.5.14. 20.15 20.8.9.19
1.18.20.9.3.12.5 6.18.15.13 20.8.5
16.1.16.5.18 20.8.5 18.9.3.8.5.19.20
3.8.9.12.4 9.14 20.8.5 23.15.18.12.4
9.19 22.9.19.9.20.9.14.7 15.21.18
20.15.23.14. 8.5.18. 14.1.13.5 9.19.
12.1.4.25 19.23.5.5.20.14.5.19.19.
6.15.18.20.5.19.3.21.5-19/13.25.20.8.5.
2.18.15.23.14.5 # 20.15.14.9.7.8 .20
8.5.18 16.1.18.5.1420.19 , 12.15.18.4
1.14.4 12.1.4.25 6-19-2 , 1.18.5
1.20.20.5.14.4.9.14.7 20.8.5 18.5.7.1.12
3.8.18.9.19.20.13.1.19 5.22.5 2.1.12.12`
`23.1. 9. 20. 9 8.1.22.5 1.14 9.4.5.1,
'19.1.9.4 3.12.15.2.2.5.18

3

List en.L et scree pove r tot her
oyalmans ion andkidna
pyou ngLad ySwe etnes s. Thenwec an
wri tear an somno
te andge trich ve ryquic kly.Bu thowc
anwekidn a pherwit
hou tbe ingc aught?
'Wa it ! I ha vean ide a's aid Do bber.

4

`Lxstxn:Xnx xf xs wxll drxss xp xs Sxntx
Clxxs. Whxt x grxxt xdxx. Nxbxdy wxll
bx xt xll sxspxcxxxs xf kxndly
Sxntx vxsxtxng x hxxsx xn Chrxstmxs
Xvx. Thx bxbysxttxr
wxll xpxn thx dxxr xnd lxt yxx xn. Yxx
cxn txll Lxdy
Swxxtnxss thxt yxx lxft hxr prxsxnts xn
thx slxxgh, xnd
thxn brxng hxr bxck hxrx.'

5

.dennalp dah srebbor eerht eht sa
yltcaxe gniog saw
gnihtyrevE .ni mih detivni dna rood eht
denepo rettis-ybab
eht noisnam lager eht ta devirra eh
nehW. emutsoc atnaS
sih ni pu desserd rebbolC sa yllufeelg
sdnah rieht deppalc
srebbor eerht ehT

6

Vg jnf nyzbfg gbb rnfl. Ynql Fjrrgarff
gbbx Pyboore'f unaq
gehfgvatylnf ur rkcynvarq gung ur unq
yrsg ure cerfragf va
gur fyrvtu. Gur onolfvggre ybbxrq
gverq naq syhfgrerq nf
fur gbyq Pyboore abg gb or va nal
uheel gb oevat Ynql
Fjrrgarff onpx ubzr.

7

'Ouch!' yelled Clobber. 'Something kicked me!' He looked around but the only person near was Lady Sweetness. All other children were in bed, waiting for Santa. Ouch! Something kicked him again. Surely it couldn't be Lady Sweetness. By the time they reached the Robbers' Cave, he was covered in bruises.

8

ehT rtheo owt sobberr delcomew mhet eomh. `sho'W that
read eittll lirg,' yhet dskea. yadL sweetness deplier yb
gickink robbeD dan rlobbeB. nheT ehs dais ot rlobbeC,`uoY reven dricket em
rof a tomenm.shere'T on hucs
nersop sa aantS. I tusj eamc glona rof eht txcitemene.'

9

Aftnr that, things bngan to go wrong with thnir plan. Lady
Swnntnnss was the worst child thny had nvnr snnn. Shn
kicknd, spat, ynllnd, sworn and brokn nvnry platn in the
cavn. Thnn shn startnd to chop up all thn furniturn.
`Hurry up and gnt that ransom notn to hnr parnnts!'
plnadnd Clobbnr and Dobbnr. Blobbnr spnd off.

10

Tyhe thrjee roblbers htad tlhe woyrst noight theiy hyad
elver explerienced. Ladly Sweretness dlidn't gto tlo saleep
ayt alti adnd delmanded tlhat theye trell hier sotories allb
nright. Shte tjore ulp ajll thyeir bookys.

Everyuthghing ihn tjhe crave waes delstroyed.
Jrust whemn threy wfere griving upp hpope thje postmqan
rofde ulp.

11

The excited robbers trembled as they opened the letter
from Lord and Lady F-S-B:
raeD, ,srebboR
eW evah dah eht tsom lufrednow samtsirhC ni rou .sevil tl
si os teiuq dna yppah tuohtiw .ssenteewS eW reven tnaw
reh .kcab
eW hsiw uoy a yrev yrrem samtsirhC dna a yppaH weN
.raeY

S.P. !aH !aH !aH
S.P.P.sevreS uoy !thgir

Hints to help solve the Crack-a-jack Christmas code story. . .

We're not going to give you even the tiniest hint for working these out. Well, O.K., if you insist, in number 6, for example,
    y n q l F j r r g a r f f,
when de-coded, is
    L a d y   S w e e t n e s s
and
    P y b o o r e becomes
    C l o b b e r
    Easy, isn't it? the other ten paragraphs are as easy as

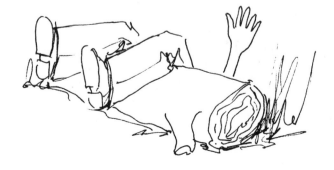

Reindeer Stencil

1 Photocopy the page and give one to each child.
2 Look at the drawing.
See that each square in the drawing is numbered.
3 Look at the box with empty squares.
See that each empty square is numbered exactly the same as the drawing.
4 Copy each part of the reindeer onto exactly the same spot and numbered square in the box.

If you copy carefully your drawing should look like the one in the picture.
5 Make several reindeers of various sizes using this method.
6 Cut out your reindeers and use them as stencils to make cards, decorate wrapping paper, windows or presents.

For a really different result use Santa Snow or spray paint to create the outline.

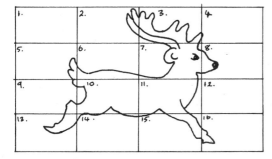

1	2	3	4
5	6	7	8
9	10	11	12
13	14	15	16

S

Santa's Savouries

Toppings and fillings

Try some different combinations for sandwiches, dry biscuits and rolls. Here are some ideas.

- Grated carrot with a squeeze of orange juice
- Sweetcorn/apple/mayonnaise
- Beetroot/plain yoghurt
- Mashed banana/cinnamon
- Banana/raisins/honey
- Chopped walnuts, cottage cheese/raisins
- Cottage cheese/pineapple
- Honey/apple slices
- Grated cheese/sliced apple
- Cheese/celery
- Mashed egg/mayonnaise
- Cheese/tomato

Cheese and parsley dip

You will need:

    230g cream cheese
    150g cream
    3 tablespoons finely chopped parsley
    juice of half a lemon
    a sprinkle of salt and pepper (if required)
    celery and carrot pieces cut in strips

1 Beat the cream cheese and the cream together in a bowl.

2 Mix in the parsley and lemon juice. Add a sprinkle of salt and pepper if you wish.

3 Put mixture in bowl and place celery and carrot pieces around the edges. (Or you could stick them in the dip — like a hedgehog's spikes!)

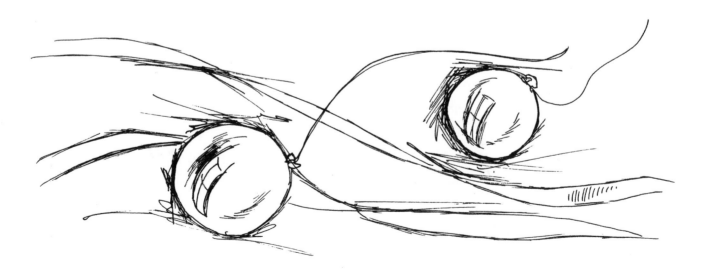

Tomato surprises

You will need:
some firm tomatoes
some tasty fillings.

1 Cut the tops off the tomatoes.

2 Hollow them out with a sharp knife or a spoon. Remove the pips and juice.

3 Fill them with interesting savoury mixtures, e.g. some nuts, raisins, and pieces of celery and apple mixed together with mayonnaise.
Try some of the topping and filling ideas on page 116.

4 Place the tops back on the tomatoes.

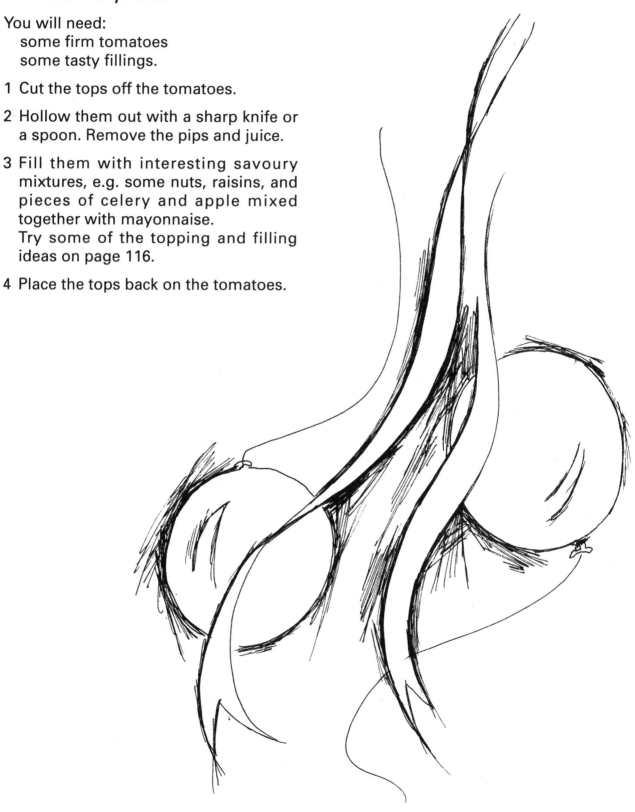

Serviette Holders

Hand-drawn holders

1 Cut a piece of firm paper, about 16cm x 8cm.

2 Draw and colour a Christmas design. (Remember the end pieces will be joined together, so don't draw to the very end!)

3 Fold your paper into a tube with the design facing out and attach the ends with tapes or staples.

4 Roll a serviette and place inside.

Decorated holders

1 Make a tube out of paper as described.

2 Cover outside surface with PVA glue. This dries quickly so it might be better to do a bit at a time.

3 Stick on designs using tiny beads, sequins or shapes.
OR use dried flowers, seeds and grasses.

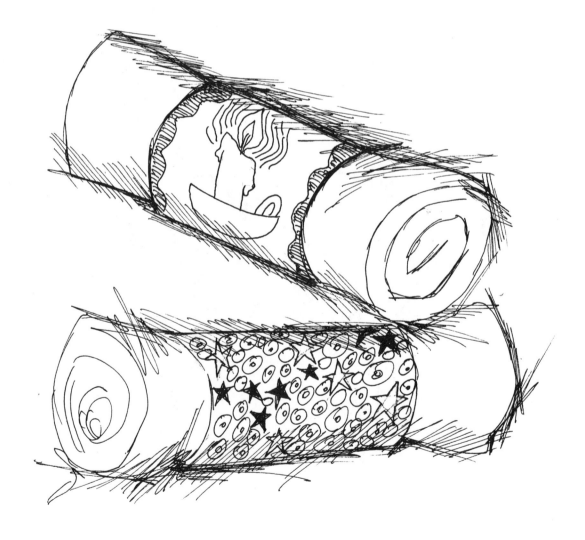

Simple Folded Cards

One-fold cards

1 Fold a piece of paper in half.

2 Draw and decorate the front and inside.

Firmer cards

1 Take a sheet of longer paper — notepad size or A4 — and fold in half.

2 Fold in half again.

3 Decorate.

Smaller Gift Cards

Attach them to the outside of presents to show who they're from.

1 Cut some small cards from board.

2 Decorate with sequins, rice, barley, buttons, felt scraps, pressed flowers.

OR you can use a leaf as a gift card. Press a leaf for a week or two in a heavy book, then write your message straight onto it.

OR you could trace round a leaf onto cardboard and cut out and make a card.

Another method is to use old Christmas cards. Cut out the parts you like and stick onto another sheet of card or paper to make your own new card.

Special Christmas Gift Vouchers

Decorate these gift vouchers and give
as a present to a special person.

Gift Voucher
TO ....
FROM...
1 AFTERNOON OF GARDENING

Gift Voucher
TO ....
FROM...
1 WEEK OF YOUR CHOICE OF T.V. PROGRAMS

Gift Voucher
TO ....
FROM...
1 WET AFTERNOON PLAYING PICTIONARY

Gift Voucher
TO ....
FROM..
1 BREAKFAST IN BED

Gift Voucher
TO ....
FROM...
3 NIGHTS OF DISHWASHING

Snowflakes

Lacy loopies

The first type is made from a square shape.

1 Fold a square diagonally three times.

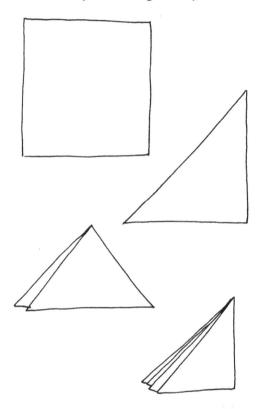

2 Cut from the folded edges, first from one side, then from the other. Leave 1cm gap at each end. (DO NOT CUT TO THE END!)

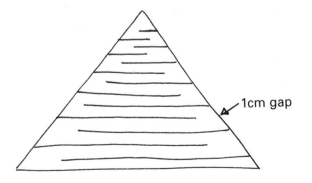

1cm gap

3 Carefully unfold the shape.

4 Pull gently and stretch it out.

5 Attach loop and hang by the smallest end.

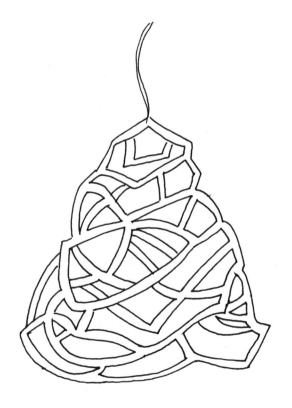

The second type is made from a circle.

1 Fold a circle of tissue or other paper in half then

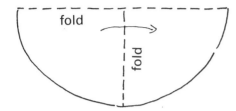

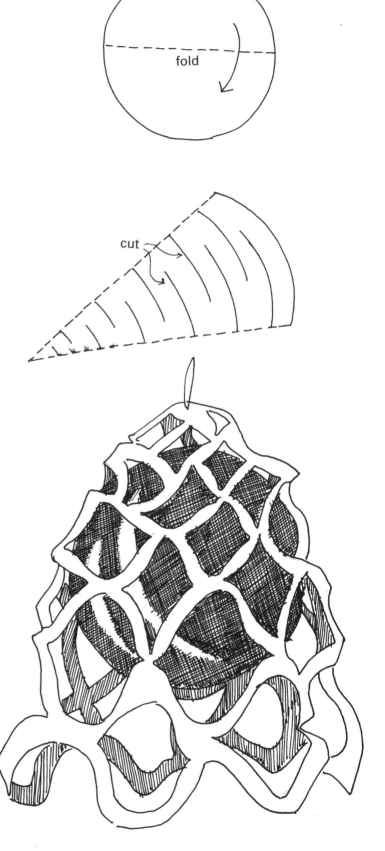

in half again.

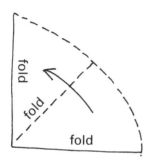

2 Cut as shown — FROM the folds, first one way, then the other.
As before — DO NOT CUT TO THE END.

3 Open out gently.
Pull apart. Attach loop.
These look effective if hung over a bright balloon.

Snowflakes

1 Fold a small square of thin paper or foil into four.

2 Fold it diagonally.

3 Cut off the unfolded edge into a curve.

4 Cut out different shapes along the folded edges. Experiment to see which shapes look best.

5 Open and hang up.

For a different effect you can stick the snowflake onto a dark-coloured piece of paper.

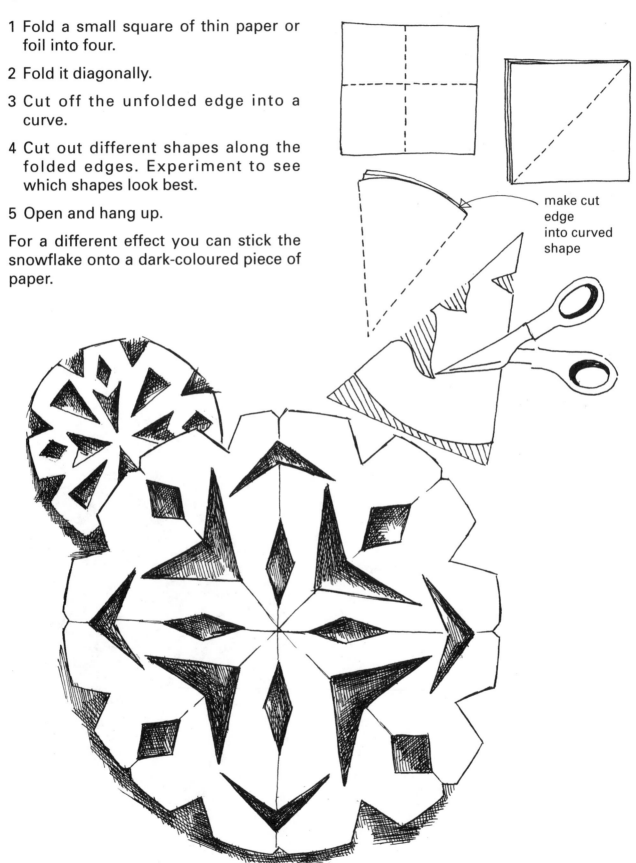

make cut edge into curved shape

Spattered Paper

We think this is far too messy, but some children we know made us write it down!

Put plenty of newspaper under the place where you're working.

1 You'll need a saucer (or small container) of paint and an old toothbrush.

2 Dip the toothbrush (don't use your everyday one!) into the paint.

3 Wipe the brush with a tissue or rub it on some old paper to get rid of extra paint. The brush should be FAIRLY DRY. This is most important!

4 Run your thumb or finger lightly over the bristles. Don't use too many colours.

5 You will get an attractive effect if you cut out stars or bells from card and place them on top of the paper before you begin.

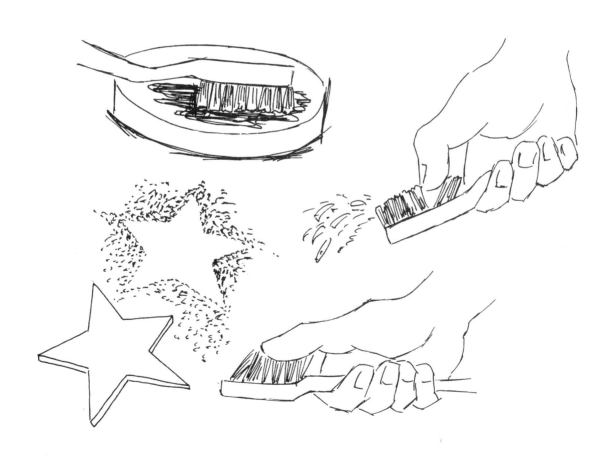

Stained Glass Window Card

You will need heavyweight paper and a pencil, a Stanley knife, scissors, coloured cellophane in various colours, and glue.

Fold the paper into quarters; then unfold.

1 Draw a church window in the bottom right-hand quarter. Then fold the top half of the paper down behind.

2 Cut out the shapes in the window, cutting through both layers of paper.

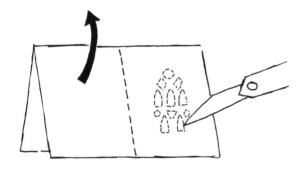

Now open up the paper.

3 Cover the cut-out areas in your window with various pieces of coloured cellophane. Glue them into place on the bottom right-hand section of the card; then close the card from top to bottom.

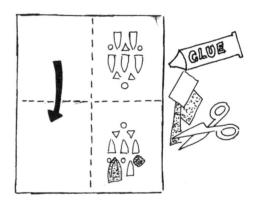

4 Then from left to right behind.

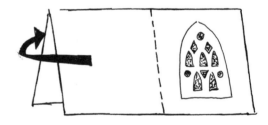

5 Complete your card by writing a Christmas message to a friend.

Stand-up Father Christmas Card

1 Cut a piece of thin card 8cm x 14cm.

2 Mark lightly with pencil as shown.

3 Fold outwards along the dotted lines.

4 Make into a triangular tube, keeping the front panel square. Stick the 2cms at the end underneath the other end (as shown).

5 Cut out the Santa shape. Colour brightly. You could use cotton wool for his beard and pom pom, and sequins for his buttons.

6 Make a name tag and message tag. Attach to each of Santa's hands (sticky tape is easier than glue).

7 If you wish, you could place a few nuts or lollies in the bottom of the tube.

8 Attach Santa to the triangular tube with glue.

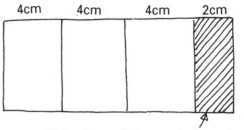

This piece will be stuck down later.

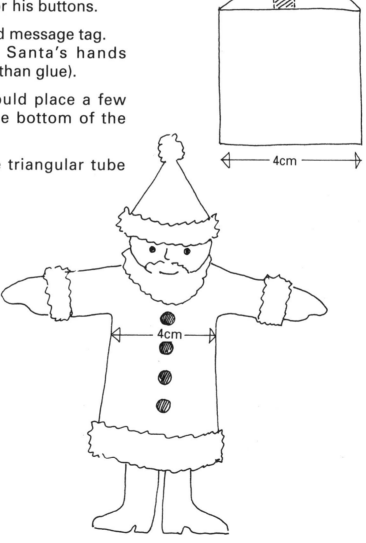

Stars

Four-pointed star

1 Cut out the square along the dotted lines. You can use this square to make your star. If you want to make more than one star use this square as a stencil.

2 Fold your square of paper in half. Open out.

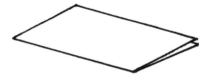

3 Now fold the other way. Open out.

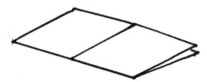

4 Fold again —

and then again.

The creases should look like this:

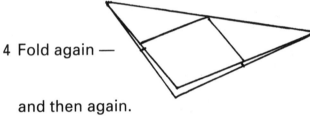

5 Now it is easy to draw your star shape on the paper.

6 Cut star out and push the middle folds out.

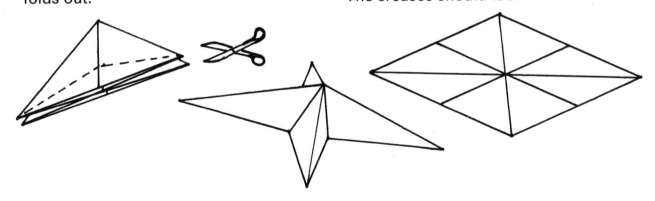

Simple five-pointed star

1 Cut star shape from thin card.

2 Cover with glue.

3 Sprinkle with glitter.

4 Use tiny stars to hange from tree, or make larger ones to hang from streamers, attached to a light-shade or wire ring.

Very easy six-pointed star

1 Cut two triangles from card or paper.

2 Turn upside down and stick to the other to make a star.

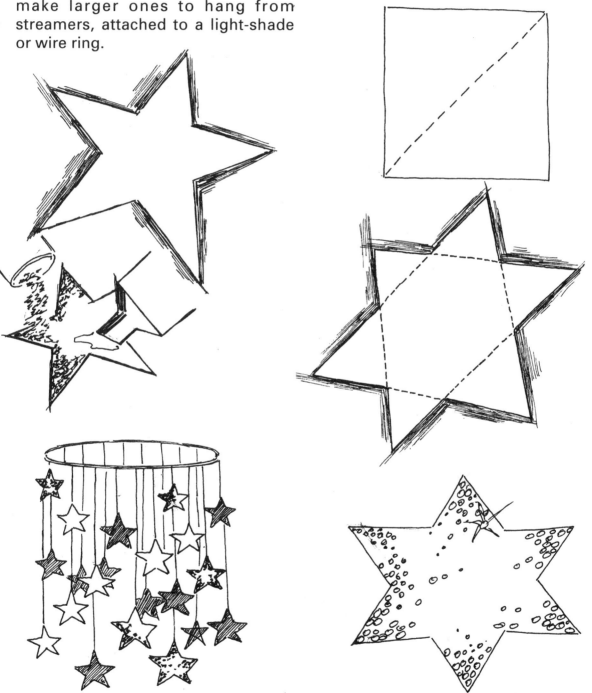

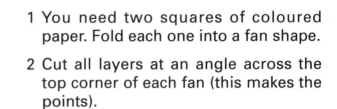

Circle stars

1 You need two squares of coloured paper. Fold each one into a fan shape.

2 Cut all layers at an angle across the top corner of each fan (this makes the points).

3 Fold one fan in half, and glue edges together. Do the same with the other fan.

4 Stick the two fans together.

glue

glue together

130

Stencilled Paper

1 Design a Christmas shape.

2 Trace onto a sheet of card and cut out design.

3 Carefully place cut-out design onto a sheet of paper.

4 Dip a paint brush into some poster paint.
Important: Squeeze brush several times between sheets of newspaper or tissue to get rid of extra paint.

5 Paint right to the very edges of your cut-out design.

6 Very gently lift the card up.

7 Wipe both sides of the stencil with a damp cloth.

8 Wait until the paint is dry before you print again.

Note: Unless your brush is very dry you will have splodges everywhere.

See what happens!
Too much paint!
(even when you're careful)

131

Stories to Read Aloud

Share these beautiful stories with your class

The Story of Silent Night

'Could you play the organ a little louder, please Franz?'

'I'm pushing the pedals as hard as I can, Father, but the notes keep on dying away.'

The two men had been rehearsing the Christmas church service for many hours. It was getting late. The creaking of the pedals grew louder and suddenly the music died away completely. There was silence. Even Franz Gruber, the finest organist in Oberndorf, couldn't coax another note from it.

Father Joseph Mohr hurried over and the two men opened a panel and peered inside the organ. In a split second the floor in front of the organ was covered with mice. Mice kept tumbling out, one after the other. The two men couldn't believe their eyes!

'Good Heavens!' shuddered the priest. Gruber pointed inside. 'Look at this, Father. No wonder those mice are so fat. They've eaten so much of the bellows that there's nothing left but rags and tatters.'

Father Mohr shook his head. The next day was Christmas Eve and he knew it was far too late to get the organ repaired in time for the Christmas service. 'A church without music', he murmured to himself. 'It is unthinkable!'

After Franz had left, the troubled priest walked outside and gazed up at the sky. The stars were brighter than he had ever remembered them, and it was so quiet that his footsteps echoed loudly. The stars reminded him of that first Christmas long ago, when that magnificent star hung low in the sky over the stable at Bethlehem. 'A long distance,' he thought, from Bethlehem

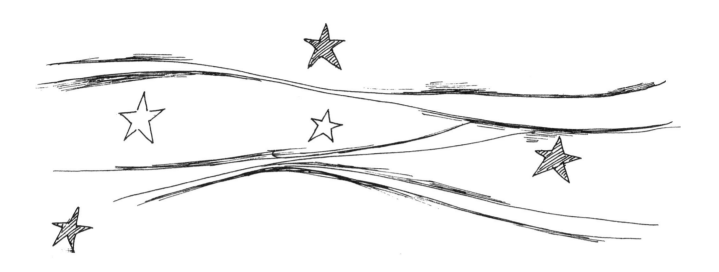

to Oberndorf, but I'm sure that the stars shine the same in both places.

Silent night, Holy night, All is calm, all is bright. . .

Father Mohr stopped in his tracks. The words seemed to sing in his mind. He ran all the rest of the way home, quickly searched for a pen and without stopping wrote these words.

Early the next morning he showed them to his organist. `It's really beautiful, Father, I can hear the words singing. Wait a moment, and I'll get my guitar.'

Franz Gruber plucked at the guitar, and soon a lovely melody began to form.

The next day Father Mohr sang the new carol while Franz Gruber accompanied him on the guitar.

The people sat in wonder. They had been bitterly disappointed when told that there would be no music in church that day, but surely this was a miracle! A beautiful new carol composed especially for them by their own village priest and their organist!

They had no idea, on that day more than a hundred and fifty years ago, that *Silent Night* — their own special carol — would travel from a little town in Austria to become the favourite carol in countries all over the world.

The Story of The Little Drummer Boy

The news of Jesus' birth spread like wildfire. It wasn't long before people from all parts of the country were planning to visit the baby, to worship him, and to bring gifts. Rich and poor, young and old, kings and shepherds — everyone wanted to see Jesus.

There were stories that if the Christ Child particularly liked you or your gift, he would smile at you and your life would be blessed from that moment on. No one was sure if that story was really true, but that was what people were saying.

In one small town lived a young boy. He had no parents and he was very poor. He slept in a shepherd's hut and earned his food by helping with the sheep. The only thing he owned was a small worn drum. Someone had thrown it out when it tore, but he had tried to mend it. He loved playing the drum. He would practice quietly for hours at the end of the day, and whenever he felt sad or lonely, his lovely music would lighten his heart.

One evening there was a loud commotion in the fields outside his hut.

`Come quickly, boy!' a shepherd called. `Some wise men are following a star which they say will lead them to a new king. We are taking our finest gifts to give to him. Come with us.'

The young shepherd hung his head. `I have no gift to bring,' he explained sadly. `The only thing I own is my drum, and I don't think a king would want that. It's very old and worn.'

All the same he decided to join the long procession. The magnificent star guided them all towards the stable. The boy had never seen so many people before. The crowd stretched right along the road, and up and down the next hill and valley. Everyone carried valuable gifts. By the time it was his turn to enter the stable he wished he had stayed home.

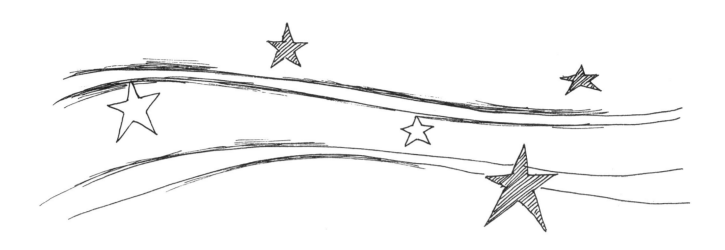

'I have nothing for the baby. I should never have come,' he whispered in despair.

At that moment Mary nodded at him, and he took out his old drum and began to play. The stable filled with music and the crowd outside became still. He played as he had never played before. He played of the hills, of the brightness of stars, of the grass and the wind. He played of his sheep, and the storms and the sun, and the loneliness of being a shepherd boy, alone with his sheep. And he played, especially, for Mary and baby Jesus.

He stopped playing, exhausted. Suddenly there was a murmur from the crowd. Baby Jesus smiled, reached out to him and touched his hand. Everyone gasped.

The boy's world seemed to fill with golden light and happiness. In a daze he stumbled from the stable.

People outside jostled to see the drummer boy. 'Are you sure that this is the boy who played so beautifully?' they asked. But they could tell there was something different about him. His lost and lonely look had vanished, and a new light of purpose shone in his face.

'Was his life blessed?' people asked, remembering the stories of times when the Christ child smiled.

Well, we can't say for sure, but there are stories about a wise teacher who travelled from place to place, telling everyone about Jesus. And we have heard that this teacher carried with him an old drum, and whenever people were sad or discouraged, he would comfort them with his music.

He brought hope into the lives of thousands of people and he lived a long, rich and rewarding life.

Table Centrepiece

Small Christmas trees

The small Christmas trees described on pages 141-144 would make a lovely centrepiece for your table.

Shell candle-holders

1 You will need a number of small shells (perhaps 6-10).

2 Cover each one in silver foil, pressing down firmly so you can see the ridges of the shell.

3 Make a base from plasticine (as above) and place a tall candle in the centre.

4 Arrange the silver shells around the base pushing them firmly into the plasticine.

Dried flower and gumnut candle-holders

1 Place a tall candle in a piece of plasticine.

2 Arrange balls, bells, baubles, dried flowers or gumnuts around the base.

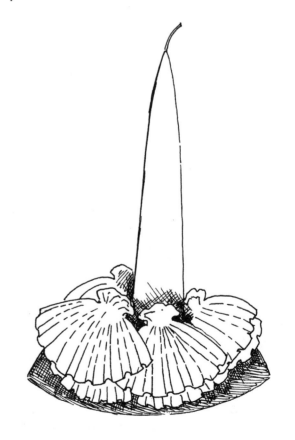

Tiny Tree Sparklers

Make these from mirrored polyester film (available from art supply shops) or you could use thin card and spray or paint them gold or silver. Or use glitter.

Christmas fishes

1 Cut out shape.

2 Cut semi-circle scales, then bend them outward.

Christmas doves

1 Cut out a dove shape from thin card.

2 Make a slit in body as shown.

3 Fold paper in a fan shape to make wings. Cut the edges as shown.

4 Push wings through the slit. Spread them out.

5 Decorate dove and hang up.

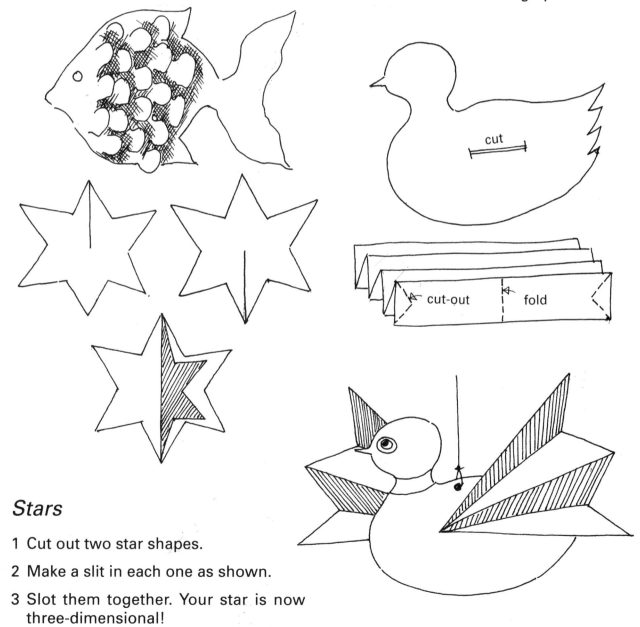

Stars

1 Cut out two star shapes.

2 Make a slit in each one as shown.

3 Slot them together. Your star is now three-dimensional!

Traditional Fare

White Christmas

You will need:

  3 cups rice bubbles
  225g copha
  1 cup dry powdered milk
  1 cup coconut
  1 cup icing sugar
  1 cup mixed fruit

1 Mix milk and sugar together.

2 Use a sifter to mix the powdered milk and icing sugar. Add to the milk and sugar.

3 Add the coconut, rice bubbles and fruit.

4 Melt the copha and add to the mixture.

5 Stir thoroughly.

6 Press mixture into a greased biscuit tray and place in fridge to set.

7 When set, cut into squares.

Uncooked chocolate log

You will need:

1 packet of Granita, Chocolate Ripple
or similar round sweet biscuits
1 small container of cream
1 teaspoon cocoa powder
1 teaspoon icing sugar

1 Put the sugar, cream and cocoa in
basin. Beat cream until it is slightly
stiff.

2 Stick the biscuits together with the
cream. (Use about half.) Put them
together, one behind the other to
make a long roll.

3 Wrap the biscuit roll in foil and place
in the fridge.

4 Leave in fridge overnight. Unwrap the
roll and spread the rest of the cream
over it. (Don't do the underneath bit.)

5 Make a bark effect on the log by
scraping a fork along.

6 Decorate with icing sugar snow, and a
sprig of plastic holly.

7 Cut small slices as this log is very
rich. Cut slices on an angle.

Simple fondants

You will need:

250g icing sugar
2 tablespoons sweetened condensed milk

1 Sift the icing sugar and mix it with the condensed milk.

2 Divide the mixture into parts to be flavoured with different essences, e.g., lemon, vanilla, peppermint.

3 Add the essence to be used to each part and mix well.

4 Add a drop of food colouring to each part, e.g., green for the peppermint, yellow for the lemon.

5 Make into small balls.

6 Coat these in coconut, chopped nuts or leave them plain.

7 Place on greaseproof paper on a tray in the fridge.

Snowballs

You will need:

55g dessicated coconut
55g plain sweet digestive biscuits or biscuits similar to digestive
55g almonds or walnuts
55g dried fruit, e.g. sultanas
75mls cream

1 Cut the fruit and nuts into very small pieces.

2 Crush the biscuits with a rolling pin.

3 Put the cut fruit and nuts and the crushed biscuits into a bowl. Add the cream. Mix thoroughly.

4 Make the mixture into balls.

5 Drop them into a bag containing the dessicated coconut. Do one or two at a time.

6 Roll them around in the bag to make the coconut stick properly.

7 Eat up!

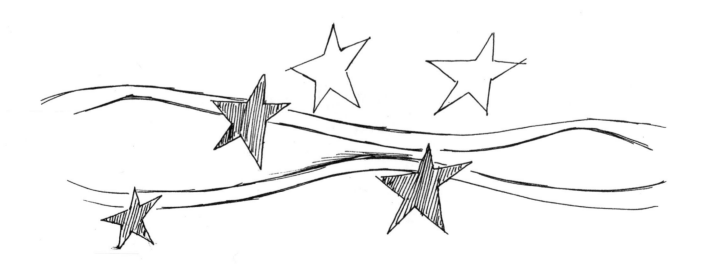

Trees for Tables

Everyone needs a Christmas tree!
If you can't get a real one, don't worry!
In this chapter, we'll show you how to
make some smaller trees.

Slotted Christmas trees

1 For a tiny Christmas tree to place in
   the centre of a table, cut out this
   pattern.

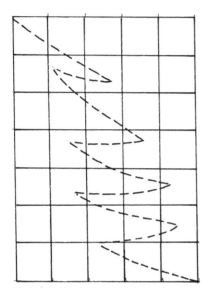

2 Unfold the pattern. Trace it onto a
   sheet of thin card.
   Make another copy. (You need two
   tree shapes.)

3 Make a slit on each tree, as shown.

4 Slot the trees together.

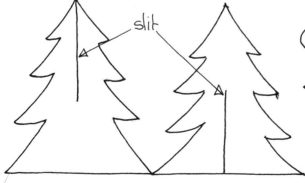

5 Make a base by cutting a strip of thin
   card 16cm long by 3cm wide. Staple
   to form circle. (This should be about
   the same size as half an empty toilet
   roll.)

6 Make four cuts in the top of the roll.

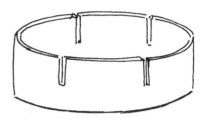

7 Fit tree into slots on base.

8 Decorate with glitter, stars and tiny
   decorations.

   (If you want a bigger tree, transfer the
   pattern onto a larger sheet of paper.
   Use the same technique as before.)

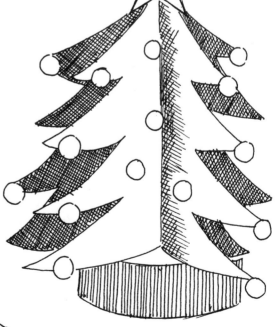

Large cardboard trees

1 Buy or find a VERY large sheet of green card. (Or buy a white piece and paint it green. Use thick poster paint.)

2 Draw a simple tree shape, then cut it out.

3 Stick decorations on. (Don't forget a glittery star on top.)

4 Prop up against a wall, or fix to the wall with Blu-tack.

Old party trick Christmas trees

1 Practise with newspaper first. (It takes a while to get the idea!)

2 You will need a roll of green crepe paper.

3 Cut 20cm length from the roll of paper. Do not unfold.

4 Cut a narrow fringe about 8cm deep.

5 Unfold the paper and place it on a table.

6 Roll it around and around a pencil. (Don't roll it too tightly.)

Keep the edges neat.

7 Take the pencil away.

Hold the fringed centre between your thumb and your first finger.

With your left hand hold the other end.

8 Pull the fringed centre upwards — very carefully.
While you are doing this, gently twist your left hand anticlockwise.
The tree will become taller and taller.

9 Pull the layers out, bit by bit.

Keep the bottom layer in place by using glue or by wrapping pipe cleaners round tightly.

10 Place tree in a small container.

Snip it. Give it a Christmassy haircut. Decorate.

11 *Sing 'O Christmas Tree'.*

O Christmas tree, O Christmas tree
How lovely are thy branches;
O Christmas tree, O Christmas tree
How lovely are they branches.
Your boughs so green in summer
    grow;
Stay evergreen through winter
    snow.
O Christmas tree, O Christmas tree
How lovely are thy branches!

O Christmas tree, O Christmas tree
You fill my heart with music;
O Christmas tree, O Christmas tree
You fill my heart with music.
So often on that merry night
When Christmas fires are burning
    bright.
O Christmas tree, O Christmas tree
How lovely are thy branches!

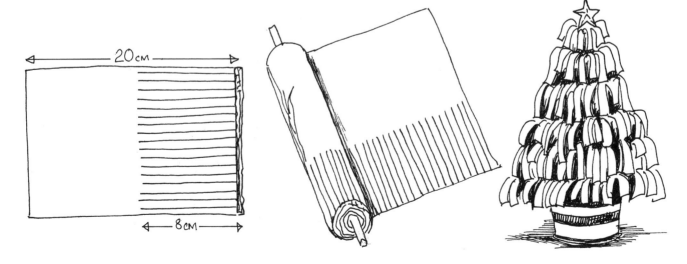

Cone tree

You will need:

polystyrene cone (from craft shop)
collection of pine cones that are not
too big
some florist's wire
coloured ribbon in Christmas colours

1 Attach a piece of wire to the base of
each pine cone.

2 Starting at the top of the polystyrene
cone press in the pine cones until the
whole tree is covered.

3 Add loops of ribbon — secured with
wire — and stuck between the cones
— to decorate the tree.

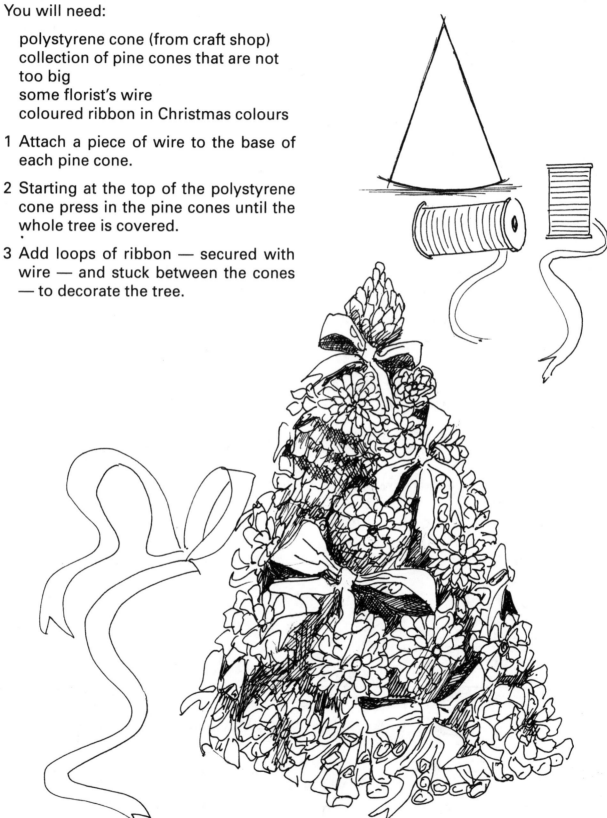

Using Marzipan

Marzipan decorations

Marzipan is a firm paste made from almonds, sugar and other ingredients.

In many countries, children use it to make models of fruit, animals or other ornaments for the Christmas tree.

For these decorations you will need a block of marzipan and some food colours.

1 Cut some pieces off and begin modelling.

2 Roll a piece into a ball.

3 Put a clove in the top.

4 Paint it to make it look like an apple.

Try an orange, a strawberry, or other shapes.

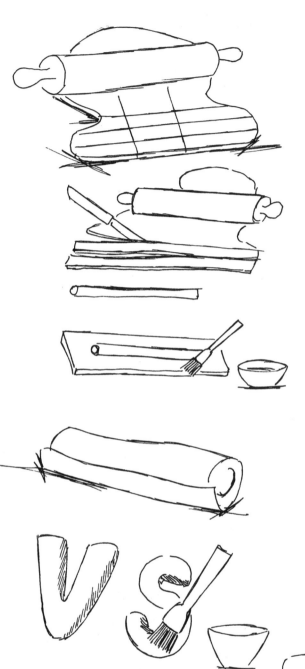

St Nicholas letters

Children in Holland and some other countries are often given St Nicholas letter biscuits on St Nicholas Day, which falls on 6 December.

You will need:

    400g frozen pastry
    200g marzipan
    1/4 cup of milk

1 Thaw pastry. Put some flour on the table and rolling pin. Roll pastry out thinly. Cut it into strips about 10cm by 4cm.

2 Roll marzipan into thin pencil shapes about 10cm long.

3 Roll the thin marzipan pencil shape up in the strips of pastry. Join them up by dabbing milk on the edges and ends.
Press firmly together.

4 Shape each roll into a letter. Seal joins with milk.

5 Place letters on a greased baking tray. Don't put them too closely together.

6 Brush tops with milk and bake for 10-15 minutes in oven 220°C .

7 Cool.

146

Wastepaper Baskets and Pencil Containers

Paint and decorate tins or boxes to make handy waste-paper baskets.

Smaller containers can hold odds and ends or pencils, pens, rulers . . .

1 Wash container.

2 Cut a sheet of paper the right size to fit around the can.

3 Paint or print your design on the paper.

4 Stick on tin using PVA glue.

5 Instead of a picture, you could do a collage design.

6 Add any other decorations you like — lace, sequins, ribbons, cut-out shapes, leaves.

7 Varnish if desired.

Window Decorations

Stained glass windows

Making a stained-glass window is far more difficult than most of the ideas in this book but the effect is so lovely that we decided to include it.

You will probably need an adult to help.

1 You will need a sheet of THICK white cardboard. (If it is too thin it warps.)

2 Work out a design. Stick to squares, rectangles, stars, triangles and diamond shapes. Circles are far too difficult.
Leave about a half a centimetre between each shape.
Rule the design onto the card.

3 Use a Stanley knife to cut out the design.
Be careful. Don't chop deeply into the card. Make a few light cutting strokes first. Then it's easier to cut deeper — your blade doesn't go skew-whiff!

4 Paint the card with black poster paint. Use a sponge roller (or a wide, thick paintbrush.)
Paint both sides.
Dry.

5 Mix PVA glue with powdered food dye in a margarine container. (Use only a tiny sprinkle of food dye — if you use too much the light can't shine through.)

6 Place the card on a sheet of plastic, and then pin to a pinboard.

7 Using a plastic spoon or a straw cut to a point, pour in a small amount of coloured PVA into every part of the design.
Plan the different colours you will use.

Use the point of the straw to push the colours into the corners of every shape in your design. Don't use too much or it will overflow.

8 Leave to dry for 24-48 hours.
Unpin card from pinboard.
Hang it in a window or where it will catch the light.

The result is spectacular.

Balloons

1 Cut out circles of different coloured cellophane.

2 Stick onto window.

3 Draw around balloon shapes with thick black felt pen.

4 Make letters by using strips of opaque sticky tape.
(Christmas sticky tape often has patterns of bells or holly and messages. This is effective because the light can't shine through.)

Candles

Use short pieces of overlapping strips of coloured cellophane to make the candle.

Bells

Cut a bell shape from coloured cellophane.
Stick it on the window with opaque stick-tape.

Bon-bons

Scrunch-up some coloured cellophane into a bon-bon shape. Stick onto window.

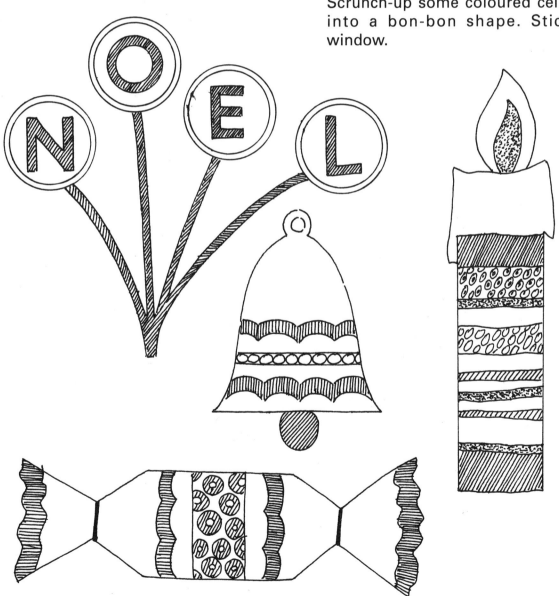

Zig Zag Cards

These are a different kind of folded card.

1 Fold some card or stiff paper into a wide fan shape.

2 Draw your design.

MAKE SURE IT TOUCHES BOTH SIDES or it will fall to bits!

3 Unfold. Trim all layers if necessary.

4 Decorate.

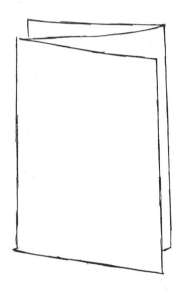

Greetings